ZEN

ZEN

*its history and teachings
and impact on humanity*

OSHO

The text material in this book is selected from various talks by Osho given
to a live audience over a period of more than thirty years. All OSHO Talks
have been published in full as books, and are also available as original
audio recordings. Audio recordings and the complete text archive can be
found via the online OSHO Library at www.osho.com
OSHO is a registered trademark of Osho International Foundation,
www.osho.com/trademarks

Picture acknowledgments
If not otherwise stated all images from the Osho International Foundation
Image Archive
The publishers would like to thank Deva Padma (www.embraceart.com)
for the illustration on p. 33;
Tenri University, Fuzoku Tenri Library, Japan, for the illustrations on pp.
58–61; and Corbis
for the top left image on p. 93.

OSHO MEDIA INTERNATIONAL
New York • Zurich • Mumbai
an imprint of
OSHO INTERNATIONAL
www.osho.com/oshointernational

Creative Director Terry Jeavons
Art Director Sarah Howerd
Commissioning Editor Mark Truman
Designer Alistair Plumb

Distributed by Publishers Group Worldwide
www.pgw.com

Library of Congress Catalog-In-Publication Data is available

Printed in India by Manipal Technologies Limited, Karnataka

ISBN 13: 978-0-9818341-6-0
ISBN 10: 0-9818341-6-7

contents

introduction

Zen is an extraordinary development. Rarely does such a possibility become an actuality because many hazards are involved. Many times before, the possibility existed—a certain spiritual happening might have grown and become like Zen, but it was never realized. Only once in the whole history of human consciousness has a thing like Zen come into being. It is very rare.

First I would like you to understand what Zen is. Try to follow me slowly through the growth of Zen—how it happened.

Zen was born in India, grew in China, and blossomed in Japan. The whole situation is rare. Why did it happen that it was born in India, but could not grow there and had to seek a different soil? It became a great tree in China, but it could not blossom there; again it had to seek a new climate, a different climate. And in Japan it blossomed like a cherry tree in thousands of flowers. It is not coincidental; it is not accidental; it has a deep inner history. I would like to reveal it to you.

India is an introverted country. Japan is extroverted. And China is just in the middle of these two extremes. India and Japan are absolute opposites. So how come the seed was born in India and blossomed in Japan? They are opposites; they have no similarities; they are contradictory. Why did China come just in the middle, to givesoil to it?

A seed is an introversion. Try to understand the phenomenon of the seed, what a seed is. A seed is an introverted phenomenon, it is centripetal—the energy is moving inward. That's why it is a seed, covered and closed from the outer world completely. In fact, a seed is the loneliest, most isolated thing in the world. It has no roots in the soil, no branches in the sky; it has no connection with the earth, no connection with the sky. It has no relationships. A seed is an absolute island, isolated, caved in. It does not relate. It has a hard shell around it; there are no windows, no doors. It cannot go out, and nothing can come in.

The seed is natural to India. The genius of India can produce seeds of tremendous potentiality, but cannot give them soil. India is an introverted consciousness. India says the outer doesn't exist, and even if it seems to exist, it is made of the same stuff that dreams are made of. The whole genius of India has been in trying to discover how to escape from the outer, how to move to the inner cave of the heart, how to be centered in oneself. And how to realize that the whole world that exists outside consciousness is just a dream—at the most beautiful, at the worst a nightmare. Whether beautiful or ugly, in reality it is a dream, and one should not bother much about it. One should awaken and forget the whole dream of the outer world.

The whole effort of Buddha, Mahavira, Tilopa, Gorakh, Kabir—their whole effort through the centuries—has been to find out how to escape from the wheel of life and death: how to enclose yourself; how to completely cut yourself off from all relationships; how to be unrelated, detached; how to move in and to forget the outer. That's why Zen was born in India.

Zen means the same as *dhyan* and is a Japanese change of this word. *Dhyan* is the whole effort of Indian consciousness, and means to be so alone, so into your own being, that not even a single thought exists. In fact, in English, there is no direct translation of the word. Contemplation is not the word. Contemplation means thinking, reflection. Even meditation is not the word because meditation involves an object to meditate upon; it means something is there. You can meditate on Christ, or you can meditate on the cross. But dhyan means to be so alone that there is nothing to meditate upon. No object, just simple subjectivity exists—consciousness without clouds, a pure sky.

When the word reached China it became *ch'an*. When *ch'an* reached Japan, it became *Zen*. It comes from the same Sanskrit root, *dhyan*.

India can give birth to dhyan. For millennia, the whole Indian consciousness has been traveling on the path of dhyan—how to drop all thinking and how to be rooted in pure consciousness. With Buddha the seed came into existence. Many times before Gautam Buddha, the seed came into existence, but it couldn't find the right soil so it disappeared. And if a seed is given to the Indian consciousness it will

“ The future of humanity will go closer to the approach of Zen, because the meeting of East and West is possible only through something like Zen, which is earthly and yet unearthly ”

disappear, because the Indian consciousness will move more and more inward, and the seed will become smaller and smaller and smaller, until a moment comes when it becomes invisible.

A centripetal force makes things smaller, smaller, smaller—atomic—until suddenly they disappear. Many times before Gautam Buddha the seed of dhyan was born—and to become a *dhyani* was to become a great meditator. In fact, Buddha is one of the last in a long series. He himself remembers twenty-four buddhas before him. Then there were twenty-four Jaina *teerthankaras*, and they all were meditators. They did nothing else, they simply meditated, meditated, meditated, until they came to a point where only they were, and everything else disappeared, evaporated.

The seed was born with Parasnath, Mahavira, Neminath, and others, but then it remained with the Indian consciousness. The Indian consciousness can give birth to a seed, but cannot become the right soil for it. It goes on working in the same direction and the seed becomes smaller and smaller, molecular, atomic—and disappears. That's how it happened with the Upanishads; that's how it happened with the Vedas; that's how it happened with Mahavira and all the others.

With Buddha it was also going to happen. Bodhidharma saved him. If the seed had been left with the Indian consciousness it would have dissolved. It would never have sprouted, because a different type of soil is needed for sprouting—a balanced soil. Introversion is a deep imbalance; it is an extreme.

Buddha himself is reported to have said, "My religion will not exist for more than five hundred years, then it will disappear." He was aware that it always happened that way. The Indian consciousness goes on grinding it into smaller and smaller and smaller pieces, then a moment comes when it becomes so small that it is invisible. It is simply no longer part of this world; it disappears into the sky.

Bodhidharma escaped with the seed to China. He did one of the greatest things in the history of consciousness: he found the right soil for the seed that Buddha had given to the world.

Bodhidharma's experiment was great. He looked and observed all around the world, deeply, for a place where this seed could grow.

China is a balanced country, not like India, not like Japan. The golden mean is the path there. Confucian ideology is to remain always in the middle: neither be an introvert nor an extrovert; neither think too much of this world nor too much of that world—just remain in the middle. China has not given birth to a religion, just to morality. No religion has been born there; the Chinese consciousness cannot give birth to a religion. It cannot create a seed. All the religions that exist in China have been imported; they have all come from the outside. Buddhism, Hinduism, Mohammedanism, and Christianity have all come from the outside. China is a good soil but it cannot originate any religion, because to originate a religion one has to move into the inner world. To give birth to a religion one has to be like a feminine body, a womb.

India is introverted, a feminine country; it is like a womb, very receptive. But if a child remains in the womb forever and forever and forever, the womb will become the grave. The child has to move out from the mother's womb, otherwise the mother will kill the child inside. He has to escape, to find the world outside, a greater world. The womb may be comfortable—it is! Scientists say we have not yet been able to create anything more comfortable than the womb. The womb is just a heaven. But even the child has to leave that heaven and come outside the mother. Beyond a certain time the

> *A seed is a miser, confined to himself, and a flower is a spendthrift*

mother can become very dangerous. Then the womb can kill, because it will have become an imprisonment. It is good for a time, when the seed is growing, but then the seed has to be transplanted to the outside world.

Bodhidharma looked around, observed the whole world, and found that China had the best soil; it was a middle ground, not extreme. The climate was not extreme, so the tree could grow easily. And China had balanced people. Balance is the right soil for something to grow: too cold is bad, too hot is bad. In a balanced climate, neither too cold nor too hot, the tree can grow.

Bodhidharma escaped with the seed, escaped with all that India had produced. Nobody was aware of what he was doing, but it was a great experiment. And he was proved right. In China, the tree grew—grew to vast proportions.

But although the tree became vaster and vaster, no flowers grew. Flowers did not come, because flowers need an extroverted country. Just as a seed is an introvert, so a flower is an extrovert. The seed is moving inward; the flower is moving outward. The flower is like male consciousness. It opens to the outer world and releases its fragrance to this outside world. Then the fragrance moves on the wings of the wind to the farthest possible corner of the world. To all directions, the flower releases the energy contained in the seed. It is a door. Flowers would like to become butterflies and escape from the tree. In fact, that is what they are doing, in a very subtle way. They are releasing the essence of the tree, the very meaning, the significance of the tree to the world. They are great sharers. A seed is a miser, confined to himself, and a flower is a spendthrift.

Japan was needed. Japan is an extroverted country. The very style of life and consciousness is extroverted. Look... in India nobody bothers about the outside world very much—about clothes, houses, the way one lives. Nobody bothers. That is why India has remained so poor. If you are not worried about the outside world, how can you become rich? If there is no concern to improve the outside world you will remain poor. And the Indian is always very serious, always getting ready to escape from life, with buddhas talking about how to become perfect dropouts from existence itself—not only from society, but ultimate dropouts from existence itself! The existence is too boring. For the Indian eye, life is just a gray color—nothing interesting in it, everything just boring, a burden. One has to carry it somehow because of past karma. Even if an Indian falls in love, he says it is because of past karma; one has to pass through it. Even love is like a burden one has to drag.

India seems to be leaning more toward death than life. An introvert has to lean toward death. That's why India has evolved all the techniques for how to die perfectly, how to die so perfectly that you are not born again. Death is the goal, not life. Life is for fools, death is for those who are wise. However beautiful a Buddha or a Mahavira may be, you will find them closed; around them a great aura of indifference exists. Whatever is happening, they are not concerned at all. Whether it happens this way or that way makes no difference; whether the world goes on living or dies, it makes no difference. In this tremendous indifference, flowering is not possible; in this inner-confined state, flowering is impossible.

Japan is totally different. With the Japanese consciousness it is as if the inner doesn't exist; only the outer is meaningful. Look at Japanese dresses. All the colors of flowers and rainbows, as if the outer is very meaningful. Look at an Indian when he is eating, and then look at the Japanese. Look at an Indian when he takes his tea, and then the Japanese. A Japanese creates a celebration out of simple things. Taking tea,

he makes it a celebration. It becomes an art. The outside is very important: clothes are very important, relationships are very important. You cannot find more outgoing people in the world than the Japanese—always smiling and looking happy. To the Indian they will look shallow; they will not look serious. Indians are the introverted people and the Japanese are the extroverts: they are opposites.

A Japanese is always moving in society. The whole Japanese culture is concerned with how to create a beautiful society, how to create beautiful relationships—in everything, in every minute thing—how to give them significance. Their houses are so beautiful. Even a poor man's house has a beauty of its own: it is artistic, it has its own uniqueness.

It may not be very rich, but still it is rich in a certain sense because of the beauty, the arrangement, the mind that has been brought to every small, tiny detail. Where the window should be, what type of curtain should be used, how the moon should be invited from the window, and from where. Very small things, but every detail is important.

To the Indian, nothing matters. If you go to an Indian temple, it is without any windows; there is nothing, no hygiene, no concern with air, ventilation—nothing. Even temples are ugly, and anything goes—dirt, dust, nobody bothers. Just in front of the temple you will find cows sitting, dogs fighting, people praying. Nobody bothers. No sense of the outer, they are not at all concerned with the outer.

Japan is very concerned with the outer—just at the other extreme. Japan was the right country. And the whole tree of Zen was transplanted in Japan, and there it blossomed in thousands of colors. It flowered.

born in
laughter

Zen is the ultimate flowering of consciousness. It started with

Gautam Buddha giving a lotus flower to Mahakashyapa.

the seed of zen

A man once took a flower and, without a word, held it up before the men seated in a circle about him. Each man in his turn looked at the flower, and then explained its meaning, its significance, all that it symbolized. The last man, however, seeing the flower, said nothing, only smiled. The man in the center then also smiled, and without a word handed him the flower. This is the origin of Zen.

BUDDHA WAS to give a talk one day, and thousands of disciples had come from miles around. When Buddha appeared he was holding a flower. Time passed, but Buddha said nothing, he just looked at the flower. The crowd grew restless, but Mahakashyap, who could restrain himself no longer, laughed. Buddha beckoned him over, handed him the flower, and said to the crowd, "All that can be given with words I have given to you; but with this flower, I give Mahakashyap the key to all the teachings."

The key to all teachings, not only for a Buddha but for all masters—Jesus, Mahavira, Lao Tzu—cannot be given through verbal communication. The key cannot be delivered through the mind; nothing can be said about it. The more you say the more difficult it becomes to deliver, because you and a buddha live in such different dimensions—not only different but diametrically opposite—that whatsoever a buddha says will be misunderstood.

I have heard that one evening three slightly deaf women met on the road. The day was very windy, so one woman said,

"Windy, isn't it?"

The other said, "Wednesday? No, it's Thursday."

And the third said, "Thirsty? I am also, so let's go to the restaurant and have a cup of tea."

This is what happens when a buddha says something to you. He says, "Windy?" You say, "Wednesday? No, it's Thursday."

The physical ear is okay, but the spiritual ear is missing. A buddha can talk only to another buddha—this is the problem—and with another buddha there is no need to talk. A buddha has to talk with those who are not enlightened. With them the need exists to talk and communicate, but then communication is impossible.

Two ignorant persons can talk. They talk much; they do nothing except talk. Two enlightened persons cannot talk—it would be absurd. Two ignorant persons talking is meaningless because there is nothing to convey. They don't know anything that can be said, that should be said, but they go on talking. They are chattering. They cannot help it; it's just a mad catharsis, a release.

Two enlightened persons cannot talk because they know the same. Nothing needs to be said. Only one enlightened person and one unenlightened person can have a meaningful communication, because one knows and the other is still in ignorance. A meaningful communication, I say. I don't say that the truth can be conveyed. But some hints, some indications, some gestures can be communicated, so that the other becomes ready to take the jump. The truth cannot be conveyed but the thirst can be given. No teaching worth the name can give the key through words.

Buddha talked—it's difficult to find another person who talked as much. Scholars have been studying all the scriptures in existence that are in the name of Buddha, and it seems an impossible accomplishment because after his enlightenment he lived only forty years, walking from one village to another.

He walked all over the province of Bihar in India, which was named Bihar because Buddha walked there. *Bihar* means the walking paths of Buddha. The whole province is called Bihar because this is the boundary where Buddha walked—his *bihar,* his wanderings.

He continually walked; only in the rainy season did he rest. So much time was wasted in walking, and then also he had to sleep. So the scholars who have been calculating say, "This seems impossible. Sleeping, walking, doing other daily routines—there are so many scriptures, how could he have talked so much? If he was continuously talking for forty years, without a gap of a single moment, only then could this much have been talked." He must have talked so much—almost continuously— yet still he says the key cannot be conveyed through words.

This story is one of the most significant, because from this was born the tradition of Zen. Buddha was the source, and Mahakashyap was the first, the original master of Zen. Buddha was the source, Mahakashyap was the first master, and this story is the source from which the whole tradition—one of the most beautiful and alive that exists on earth, the tradition of Zen—started.

Try to understand this story. Buddha came one morning and, as usual, a crowd had

gathered; many people were waiting to listen to him. But one thing was unusual—he was carrying a flower in his hand. Never before had he carried anything in his hand. People thought that someone must have presented it to him. Buddha came; he sat under the tree. The crowd waited and waited and he did not speak. He wouldn't even look at them, he just went on looking at the flower. Minutes passed, then hours, and the people became very restless.

It is said that Mahakashyap couldn't contain himself. He laughed out loud. Buddha called him, gave him the flower and said to the gathered crowd, "Whatsoever can be said through words I have said to you, and that which cannot be said through words I give to Mahakashyap. The key cannot be communicated verbally. I hand over the key to Mahakashyap."

This is what Zen masters call "transference of the key without scripture"—beyond scripture, beyond words, beyond mind. He gave the flower to Mahakashyap, and nobody could understand what happened. Neither Mahakashyap nor Buddha ever commented upon it again. The whole chapter was closed. Since then, in China, in Tibet, in Thailand, in Burma, in Japan, in Ceylon—everywhere— Buddhists have been asking for these twenty-five centuries, "What was given to Mahakashyap? What was the key?"

The whole story seems to be very esoteric. Buddha was not secretive; this was the only incident…. Buddha was a very rational being. He talked rationally, he was not a mad ecstatic, he argued rationally, and his logic was

perfect—you could not find a loophole in it. This was the only incident where he behaved illogically, where he did something that was mysterious. He was not a mysterious man at all. You cannot find another master who was less mysterious.

Jesus was very mysterious. Lao Tzu was absolutely mysterious. Buddha was plain, transparent; no mystery surrounds him, no smoke is allowed. His flame burns clear and bright, absolutely transparent, smokeless. This was the only thing that seemed mysterious; hence many Buddhist scriptures never relate this anecdote; they have simply dropped it. It seemed as if someone had invented it. It didn't make any sense with Buddha's life and teaching.

But for Zen this is the origin. Mahakashyap became the first holder of the key. Then six holders of the key lived in succession in India, up through Bodhidharma, who was the sixth holder of the key.

To me, if all the scriptures of Buddha disappear nothing is lost. Only this anecdote should not disappear. This is the most precious, yet scholars have dropped it from Buddha's biography. They say, "This is irrelevant; it doesn't fit with Buddha." But I say to you, most of what Buddha did was just ordinary, anybody could do it, but this is extraordinary, this is exceptional. Only a buddha can do this.

What happened that morning? Let us penetrate into it. Buddha came, sat, and started looking at the flower. What was he doing? When Buddha looks at anything, the quality of his consciousness is transferred. And a flower is one of the most receptive things in the world. Hence, Hindus and Buddhists go with flowers to put at their master's feet or in the temple, because a flower can carry something of your consciousness.

A flower is receptive and, if you are aware of the new research in the West, you will understand it. Now they say plants are more sensitive than human beings. A flower is the heart of the plant; the whole being comes into it. Much research is going on in Russia, in the

US, in the UK, about the sensitivity of plants, and something wonderful has been discovered.

One man, a scientist, was studying plants—how they feel, whether they feel anything or not, whether they have emotions or not. He was sitting with a plant with electrodes fixed to it to detect any movement in its inner being, any sensation, any emotion. He thought, "If I cut this plant, if I tear down a branch or cut it from the earth, what will happen?" Suddenly, the needle writing the graph jumped. He had not done anything, he had just had a thought: "If I cut this plant...." The plant became afraid of death and the needle jumped, recording that the plant was trembling. Even the scientist became frightened because he had not done anything—just a thought and the plant received it. Plants are telepathic.

Not only this, but if you think of cutting one plant, all the other plants surrounding the area become emotionally disturbed. Also, if someone has cut a plant and he comes into the garden, all the plants become disturbed because this man is not good and they carry the memory. Whenever this man enters the garden the whole garden feels that a dangerous person is coming in. Now a few scientists think that plants can be used for telepathic communication, because they are more sensitive than the human mind.

In the East it has always been known that a flower is the most receptive thing. When Buddha looked at the flower and continued to look at the flower, something of him was transferred to that flower. Buddha entered the flower. The quality of his being—the alertness, the awareness, the peace, the ecstasy, the inner dance—touched the flower. With Buddha looking at the flower—so at ease, at home, without any desire—the flower must have danced in its inner being. Buddha looked in order to transfer something to the flower. Only the flower and he existed—for a long period of time, the whole world dropped. Only Buddha and the flower were there. The flower entered Buddha's being, and Buddha entered the flower's being.

Then the flower was given to Mahakashyap. It was not just a flower now. It carried buddhahood; it carried the inner quality of Buddha's being. And why to Mahakashyap? There were other great scholars. History records ten great disciples; Mahakashyap was only one, and he was included in the ten only because of this story; otherwise, he would never have been included.

Nothing much is known about Mahakashyap. Great scholars like Sariputta were there—you could not find a more keen intellect. Moggalayan was also there; a great scholar, he had all the Vedas in his memory, and nothing that had ever been written was unknown to him. A great logician in his own right, he had thousands of disciples. And there were others. Ananda was there, Buddha's cousin-brother, who for forty years was continuously moving with him. But no, someone who was unknown before—Mahakashyap—suddenly became very important. The whole gestalt changed. Whenever Buddha was speaking, Sariputta was the significant man because he could understand words more than anybody else, and when Buddha was arguing, Moggalayan was the significant man. Nobody thought about Mahakashyap very much. He remained in the crowd, was part of the crowd.

But when Buddha became silent, the whole gestalt changed. Now Moggalayan and Sariputta were not significant; they simply dropped out of existence as if they were not there. They became part of the crowd. A new man, Mahakashyap, became the most important. A new dimension opened. Everybody was restless, thinking, "Why is Buddha not speaking? Why is he keeping silent? What is going to happen? When will it end?" They became uncomfortable, restless.

But Mahakashyap was not uncomfortable or restless. Instead, for the first time he was at ease with Buddha; for the first time he was at home with Buddha. When Buddha was talking he may have been restless. He may have thought, "Why this nonsense? Why go on talking? Nothing is conveyed, nothing is understood; why go on knocking your head against the wall? People are deaf. They cannot understand...." He must have been restless when Buddha was talking, and now for the first time he was at home. He could understand what silence was.

Thousands were there and everybody was restless. He couldn't contain himself, looking at the foolishness of the crowd. They were at ease when Buddha was talking; now they were restless when he was silent. When something could be delivered they were not open; when

nothing could be delivered they were waiting. Through silence Buddha could give something immortal, but they could not understand. So he couldn't contain himself and laughed aloud—he laughed at the situation, the absurdity.

Mahakashyap laughed at the foolishness of people. They were restless and thinking, "When will Buddha stand up and drop this whole silence so that we can go home?" He laughed. Laughter started with Mahakashyap and has been going on and on in the Zen tradition. There is no other tradition that can laugh. Laughter looks so irreligious, profane, that you cannot think of Jesus laughing, you cannot think of Moses laughing. It's difficult even to conceive of Moses having a belly laugh, or of Jesus laughing uproariously. No, laughter has been denied. Sadness, somehow, has become religious.

One of the famous German thinkers, Count Keyserling, has written that health is irreligious. Illness has a religiousness about it because an ill person is sad, desireless—not because he has become desireless, but because he is weak. A healthy person will laugh, wants to enjoy, will be merry—he cannot be sad. So religious people have tried in many ways to make you ill: go on a fast, suppress your body, torture yourself. You will become sad, suicidal, crucified on your own. How can you laugh? Laughter comes out of health. It's an overflowing energy. That's why children can laugh and their laughter is total. Their whole body is involved in it—when they laugh you can see their toes laughing. The whole body—every cell, every fiber of the body—is laughing

and vibrating. They are so full of health, so vital; everything is flowing.

A sad child is an ill child and a laughing old man is still young. Even death cannot make him old; nothing can make him old. His energy is still flowing and overflowing; he is always flooded. Laughter is a flooding of energy.

In Zen monasteries they have been laughing and laughing and laughing. Laughter becomes prayer only in Zen, because Mahakashyap started it. Twenty-five centuries ago, on a morning just like this, Mahakashyap started a new trend, absolutely new, unknown to the religious mind before—he laughed. He laughed at the foolishness, the stupidity. And Buddha didn't condemn him; on the contrary, he called him near, gave him the flower, and spoke to the crowd.

And when the crowd heard the laughter they must have thought, "This man has gone mad. This man is disrespectful to Buddha, because how can you laugh in front of a buddha? When a buddha is sitting silently, how can you laugh? This man is not paying respect."

The mind will say that this is disrespect. The mind has its rules, but the heart does not know them; the heart has its own rules, but the mind has never heard about them. The heart can laugh *and* be respectful. The mind cannot laugh, it can only be sad and then be respectful. But what kind of respect is this, which cannot laugh? A new trend entered with Mahakashyap's laughter, and down the centuries the laughter has continued.

Only Zen masters and Zen disciples laugh. All over the world, religions have become ill because sadness has become so prominent. Temples and churches look like graveyards; they don't look festive, they don't give a sense of celebration. If you enter a church, what do you see there? Not life, but death— Jesus crucified on the cross completes the sadness there. Can you laugh in a church, dance in a church, sing in a church? Yes, there is singing, but it is sad and people sit with long faces. No wonder nobody wants to go to church—it's just a social duty to be fulfilled. No wonder nobody is attracted to the church—it is a formality. Religion has become a Sunday thing. For one hour you can tolerate being sad.

Mahakashyap laughed in front of Buddha and since then the Zen monks and masters have been doing things that so-called religious minds cannot even conceive. If you have seen any Zen book you may have seen Zen masters depicted or painted. No painting is realistic. If you look at Bodhidharma's portrait or Mahakashyap's portrait, they are not true to their faces, but just looking at them you will have a feeling of laughter. They are hilarious; they are ridiculous.

Look at Bodhidharma's pictures. He must have been one of the most beautiful men; that he was otherwise is not possible, because whenever a man becomes enlightened a beauty descends, a beauty that comes from the beyond. A blessing comes to his whole being. But look at Bodhidharma's picture. He looks ferocious and dangerous. He looks so dangerous that you will be scared if he comes to visit you in the night—never again in your life will you be able to sleep! He looks so dangerous, as if he is going to kill you. It was just disciples laughing at the master, creating a ridiculous portrait that looks like a cartoon.

Silence and laughter are the keys

—silence within,

laughter without

All Zen masters are depicted in a ridiculous way. Disciples enjoy it. But those portraits carry a message that Bodhidharma is dangerous, that if you go to him he will kill you, that you cannot escape him, that he will follow you and haunt you. Wherever you go, he will be there; unless he kills you he cannot leave you. That is the message depicted with all Zen masters, even Buddha.

If you look at Japanese and Chinese paintings of Buddha, they don't look like the Indian Buddha. They have changed him totally. If you look at Indian paintings of Buddha, his body is proportionate, as it should be. He was a prince, then a buddha—a beautiful man, perfect, proportionate. A big-bellied Buddha? He never had a big belly. But in Japan, in his paintings and his scriptures, he is painted with a big belly because a man who laughs must have a big belly. Belly laughter—how can you do it with a small belly? You cannot do it. They are joking with Buddha and they have said such things about Buddha. Only very deep love can do that, otherwise it looks insulting.

The Zen master Bankei always insisted on having a painting of Buddha hanging behind him, and talking to his disciples he would say, "Look at this fellow. Whenever you meet him, kill him immediately; don't give him a chance. While meditating he will come to disturb you. Whenever you see his face in meditation, just kill him then and there; otherwise, he will follow you." And he used to say, "Look at this fellow! If you repeat his name"—because Buddhists go on repeating, *Namo Buddhaya, namo Buddhaya*—"if you

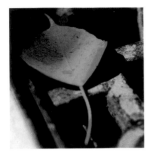  

repeat his name, then go and wash your mouth." This statement seems insulting. It is Buddha's name and Bankei says, "If you repeat it, the first thing to do is wash your mouth. Your mouth has become dirty."

But he is right—because words are words; whether one is the name of Buddha or not makes no difference. Whenever a word crosses your mind, your mind has become dirty. Wash out even Buddha's name.

And this man, keeping the portrait of Buddha always behind him, would bow down to it every morning. So his disciples asked, "What are you doing? You go on telling us to kill this man, not to allow him to stand in the way. You say, 'Don't take his name; don't repeat it; if it comes to you, wash out your mouth.' And now we see you bowing down to him!"

Bankei said, "All this has been taught to me by this fellow, so I have to pay him respect."

Mahakashyap laughed—and his laughter carried many dimensions within it. In the second dimension, laughter at the foolishness of the whole situation, at the Buddha silent and nobody understanding him, everybody

expecting him to speak. His whole life Buddha had been saying that the truth cannot be spoken, and still everybody expected him to speak. In the second dimension, he laughed at Buddha also, at the whole dramatic situation he had created, sitting there with a flower in his hand, looking at the flower, creating so much uneasiness and restlessness in everybody. At this dramatic gesture of Buddha he laughed and he laughed.

The third dimension was to laugh at his own self. Why couldn't he understand before now? The whole thing was easy and simple. And the day you understand, you will laugh too, because there is nothing to be understood. There is no difficulty to be solved. Everything has always been simple and clear. How could you miss it?

With Buddha sitting silent, the birds singing in the trees, the breeze passing through, and everybody restless, Mahakashyap understood. What did he understand? He understood that there is nothing to be understood, there is nothing to be said, there is nothing to be explained. The whole situation is simple and transparent.

Nothing is hidden in it. There is no need to search, because all that is, is here and now, within you. He laughed at his own self also, at the whole absurd effort of many lives just to understand this silence—he laughed at so much thinking.

Buddha called him, gave him the flower, and said, "Hereby, I give you the key." What is the key? Silence and laughter are the keys—silence within, laughter without. And when laughter comes out of silence, it is not of this world; it is divine.

When laughter comes out of thinking it is ugly; it belongs to this ordinary, mundane world; it is not cosmic. Then you are laughing at somebody else, at somebody else's cost, and it is ugly and violent.

When laughter comes out of silence you are not laughing at anybody's cost, you are simply laughing at the whole cosmic joke. And it really is a joke! That's why I go on telling jokes...because jokes carry more than any scriptures. It is a joke because inside you, you have everything—yet you are searching everywhere! What else should a joke be? You are a king and acting like a beggar in the streets—not only acting, not only deceiving others, but also deceiving yourself that you are a beggar. You have the source of all knowledge and you are asking questions; you have the knowing self and think that you are ignorant; you have the deathless within you and are afraid and fearful of death and disease. This really is a joke, and if Mahakashyap laughed, he did well.

But, except for Buddha, nobody understood. He accepted the laughter and immediately realized that Mahakashyap had attained. The quality of that laugh was cosmic; he understood the whole joke of the situation. There was nothing else to it. The whole thing is as if the divine is playing hide-and-seek with you. Others thought Mahakashyap was a fool, laughing in front of Buddha. But Buddha thought this man had become wise. Fools always have a subtle wisdom in them, and the wise always act like fools.

In the old days all great emperors always had one fool in their court. They had many wise men, counselors, ministers, and prime ministers, but always one fool. Even though many of them were intelligent and wise, emperors all over the world in the East and the West had a court jester, a fool. Why? Because there are things so-called wise men will not be able to understand, that only a foolish man can understand, because the wise can be so foolish that their cunningness and cleverness close their minds.

A fool is simple, and was needed because many times the so-called wise would not say something because they were afraid of the emperor. A fool is not afraid of anybody else. He will speak whatsoever the consequences. A fool is a man who will not think of the consequences. A clever man always thinks first of the result, then he acts. Thought comes first, then action. A foolish man acts; thought never comes first. Whenever someone realizes the ultimate, he is not like a wise man. He cannot be. He may be like a fool but he cannot be like a wise man. When Mahakashyap laughed he was a fool, and Buddha understood him. Later on, Buddhist priests didn't understand him, so they dropped the anecdote.

This anecdote has been dropped from Buddhist scriptures because it is sacrilegious to laugh before Buddha. To make it the original source of a great tradition as Zen is not good. This is not a good precedent that a man laughed before Buddha, and also not a good thing that Buddha gave the key to this man and not to Sariputta, Ananda, Moggalayan, and others who were important, significant. And finally, it was they, Sariputta, Ananda, and Moggalayan, who recorded the scriptures.

Mahakashyap was never asked. Even if they had asked he would not have answered. Mahakashyap was never consulted whether he had something to say to be recorded.

When Buddha died, all the monks gathered and started recording what happened and what did not. Nobody asked Mahakashyap. This man must have been discarded by the community. The whole community must have felt jealous. The key had been given to this man who was not known at all, who was not a great scholar or pundit. Nobody knew him before, and suddenly that morning he became the most significant man because of the laughter, because of the silence.

And in a way they were right, because how can you record silence? You can record words, you can record what happened in the visible, but how can you record what has not happened in the visible? They knew the flower had been given to Mahakashyap, nothing else.

But the flower was just a container. It had something in it—buddhahood, the touch of Buddha's inner being, the fragrance that cannot be seen, that cannot be recorded. The whole thing seems as if it never happened, or as if it happened in a dream.

Those who recorded the scriptures were men of words, proficient in verbal communication, in talking, discussing, arguing. But Mahakashyap is never heard of again. This is the only thing known about him, such a small thing that the scriptures must have missed it. Mahakashyap has remained silent, and silently the inner river has been flowing. To others the key has been given, and the key is still alive, it still opens the door.

These two are the parts: the inner silence—the silence so deep that there is no vibration in your being; you are, but there are no waves; you are just a pool without waves, not a single wave arises; the whole being silent, still; inside, at the center, silence—and on the periphery, celebration and laughter. Only silence can laugh, because only silence can understand the cosmic joke.

So your life becomes a vital celebration, your relationship becomes a festive thing. Whatsoever you do, every moment is a festival. You eat, and eating becomes a celebration; you take a bath, and bathing becomes a celebration; you talk, and talking becomes a celebration. Relationship becomes a celebration. Your outer life becomes festive; there is no sadness in it. How can sadness exist with silence? But ordinarily you think otherwise: you think if you are silent you will be sad.

Ordinarily you think, how can you avoid sadness if you are silent? I tell you that the silence that exists with sadness cannot be true. Something has gone wrong. You have missed the path; you are off the track. Only celebration can give proof that a real silence has happened.

Buddha must have known Mahakashyap. He must have known when he was looking at the flower silently and everybody was restless, he must have known that only one being there, Mahakashyap, was not restless.

Buddha must have felt the silence coming from Mahakashyap, but he would not call him up. When he laughed, then Buddha called him and gave him the flower. Why? Silence is only the half of it.

Mahakashyap would have missed if he had been innocently silent and didn't laugh. Then the key would not have been given to him. He was only half grown, not yet a fully grown tree, not blossoming. The tree was there, but flowers had not yet come. Buddha waited.

Now, I will tell you why Buddha waited for so many minutes, why for one or two or three hours he waited.

Mahakashyap was silent but he was trying to contain laughter, he was trying to control laughter. He was trying not to laugh because it would be so unmannerly: What would Buddha think? What would the others think? But then, the story says, he couldn't contain himself anymore. It had to come out as a laugh. The flood became too much, and he couldn't contain it anymore.

When silence is too much it becomes laughter; it becomes so overflooded that it starts overflowing in all directions. He laughed. It must have been a mad laughter, and in that laughter there was no Mahakashyap. Silence was laughing; silence had come to a blossoming.

Then immediately Buddha called Mahakashyap: "Take this flower—this is the key. I have given to all others what can be given in words, but to you I give that which cannot be given in words. The message beyond words, the most essential, I give to you."

Buddha waited for those hours so that Mahakashyap's silence could overflow and become laughter.

the lion's
roar

Bodhidharma did one of the greatest things in the history of consciousness: he found the right soil for the seed that Buddha had given to the world.

bodhidharma goes to china

In these fourteen centuries that have followed Bodhidharma, hundreds of Zen masters of great clarity, insight and awakening, have appeared, but no one even comes close to the depth, the subtlety, the beauty, and the immense perception of Bodhidharma. As I look into Bodhidharma, I don't find any other single individual in the whole history of mankind—Gautam Buddha included—who can be said to have condensed religion into its simplest possibility, expressed religion into its absolute purity. It is obvious that this man is going to be misunderstood, condemned, ignored. The greatest peak of consciousness that man has achieved, mankind has not been kind enough to remember. Perhaps there are heights our eyes cannot see, but we should try our best. One never knows.

BODHIDHARMA WAS BORN fourteen centuries ago as a son of a king in the south of India where there was a big empire, the empire of Pallavas. He was the third son of his father. But seeing everything—he was a man of tremendous intelligence—he renounced the kingdom. He was not against the world, but he was not ready to waste his time in mundane affairs, in trivia.

His whole concern was to know his self-nature, because without knowing it, you have to accept death as the end. All true seekers, in fact, have been fighting against death. Bertrand Russell has said that if there were no death, there would be no religion. There is some truth in this. I will not agree totally, because religion is a vast continent. It is not only a response to death, it is also the search

for bliss, it is also the search for truth, and it is also the search for the meaning of life. It is many more things. But certainly Bertrand Russell is right: if there were no death, very few, very rare people would be interested in religion. Death is a great incentive.

Bodhidharma renounced the kingdom, saying to his father, "If you cannot save me from death, then please don't prevent me. Let me go in search of something that is beyond death."

Those were beautiful days, particularly in the East. The father thought for a moment and he said, "I will not prevent you, because I cannot prevent your death. You go on your search with all my blessings. It is sad for me but that is my problem; it is my attachment. I was hoping for you to be my successor, to be the emperor of the great Pallavas empire, but you have chosen

something higher than that. I am your father, so how can I prevent you? And you have put in such a simple way a question which I had never expected. You say, 'If you can prevent my death, then I will not leave the palace. But if you cannot prevent my death, then please don't prevent me from leaving, either.'"

You can see Bodhidharma's great intelligence. And although he was a follower of Gautam Buddha, in some instances he shows higher flights than Gautam Buddha himself. For example, Gautam Buddha was afraid to initiate a woman into his commune of disciples, but Bodhidharma was initiated by a woman who was enlightened. Her name was Pragyatara. Perhaps people would have forgotten her name; it is only because of Bodhidharma that her name still remains known. But only the name—we don't know anything else about her. It was she who ordered Bodhidharma to go to China.

Buddhism had reached China six hundred years before Bodhidharma. It was something magical; it had never happened anywhere, at any time, and Buddha's message immediately caught hold of the whole Chinese people. The situation was such that China had lived under the influence of Confucius and was tired of it because Confucius was just a moralist, a puritan. He did not know anything about the inner mysteries of life.

There were people like Lao Tzu, Chuang Tzu, and Lieh Tzu, contemporaries of Confucius, but they were mystics, not masters. They could not create a counter-movement against Confucius in the hearts of the Chinese people. So there was a vacuum. Nobody can live without a soul, and once you start thinking that there is no soul, your life starts losing all meaning. The soul is your integrating concept; without it you are cut away from existence and eternal life. Just like a branch cut from a tree is bound to die—it has lost the source of nourishment—the very idea that there is no soul inside you, no consciousness, cuts you away from existence. One starts shrinking; one starts feeling suffocated.

Confucius was a great rationalist. These mystics—Lao Tzu, Chuang Tzu, Lieh Tzu— knew that what Confucius was doing was

wrong, but they were not masters. They remained in their monasteries with their few disciples.

When Buddhism reached China, it immediately entered into the very soul of the people, as if they had been thirsty for centuries and Buddhism had come as a rain cloud. It quenched their thirst so immensely that something unimaginable happened. Buddhism simply explained itself, and the beauty of the message was understood by the people. They were thirsty for it; they were waiting for something like it. The whole country, which was the biggest country in the world, turned to Buddhism. When Bodhidharma arrived six hundred years later, there were already thirty thousand Buddhist temples, monasteries, and two million Buddhist monks in China. Two million Buddhist monks is not a small number; it was five percent of the whole population of China.

Pragyatara, Bodhidharma's master, told him to go to China because the people who had reached there before him had made a great impact, although none of them were enlightened. They were great scholars, disciplined people, loving and peaceful and compassionate, but none of them were enlightened. And now China needed another Gautam Buddha. The ground was ready.

Bodhidharma was the first enlightened man in the Buddhist tradition to reach China. There are many legends about the man; they all have some significance. The first legend is that when he reached China—it took him three years— the Chinese emperor, Wu, came to receive him.

Bodhidharma's fame had preceded him. Emperor Wu had done great service to the philosophy of Gautam Buddha. Thousands of scholars were translating Buddhist scriptures from Pali into Chinese, and the emperor was the patron of that great work of translation. He had built thousands of temples and monasteries, and he was feeding thousands of monks. He had put his whole treasure in the service of Gautam Buddha.

Naturally, the Buddhist monks who had arrived before Bodhidharma had been telling the emperor that he was earning great virtue, that he would be born as a god in heaven. So his first question to Bodhidharma was, "I have made so many monasteries, I am feeding thousands of scholars, I have opened a university for the studies of Gautam Buddha, I have put my whole empire and its treasures in the service of Gautam Buddha. What is going to be my reward?"

He was a little taken aback seeing Bodhidharma, not having thought that the man would be like this. He looked ferocious. He had very big eyes, but a very soft heart—just a lotus flower in his heart. But his face was as dangerous looking as you can conceive. Just the sunglasses were missing; otherwise he looked like a Mafia guy! With great fear, Emperor Wu asked the question, and Bodhidharma said, "Nothing, no reward. On the contrary, be ready to fall into the seventh hell."

The emperor said, "But I have not done anything wrong—why the seventh hell? I have been doing everything that the Buddhist monks have been telling me."

Bodhidharma said, "Unless you start hearing your own voice, nobody can help you, Buddhist or non-Buddhist. And you have not yet heard your inner voice. If you had heard it, you would not have asked such a stupid question.

"On the path of Gautam Buddha there is no reward because the very desire for reward comes from a greedy mind. The whole teaching of Gautam Buddha is desirelessness. And if you are doing all these so-called virtuous acts—making temples and monasteries and feeding thousands of monks—with a desire in your mind, you are preparing your way to hell. If you are doing these things out of joy, to share your joy with the empire, and there is not even a slight desire anywhere for any reward, the very act is a reward unto itself. Otherwise you have missed the whole point."

Emperor Wu said, "My mind is so full of thoughts. I have been trying to create some peace of mind, but I have failed and because of these thoughts and their noise, I cannot hear what you are calling the inner voice. I don't know anything about it."

Bodhidharma said, "Then at four o'clock in the morning, come alone without any bodyguards to the temple in the mountains where I am going to stay. And I will put your mind at peace, forever."

The emperor thought, "This man is really outlandish, outrageous!" He had met many monks; they were so polite, but, "This one does not even bother that I am an emperor of a great country. And to go to him in the darkness

"Strange, because I have been asking," the emperor thought, "of many wise people who have come from India, and they all gave me methods, techniques, which I have been practicing, but nothing is happening. And this strange fellow, who looks almost mad, or drunk, and has a strange face with such big eyes that he creates fear.... But he seems to be sincere too. He is a wild phenomenon! It is worth the risk. What can he do? At the most he can kill me." Finally, he could not resist the temptation to go, because the man had promised, "I will put your mind at peace forever."

Emperor Wu reached the temple at four o'clock, early in the morning in darkness, alone, and Bodhidharma was standing there with his staff, just on the steps. He said, "I knew you would be coming, although the whole night you debated whether to go or not to go. What kind of an emperor are you? So cowardly, being afraid of a poor monk, a poor beggar who has nothing in the world except this staff. And with this staff I am going to put your mind to silence."

The emperor thought, "My God, who has ever heard that with a staff you can put somebody's mind to silence! You can finish him, hit him hard on the head—then the whole man is silent, not just the mind. But now it is too late to go back."

And Bodhidharma said, "Sit down here in the courtyard of the temple." There was not a single person around. "Close your eyes. I am sitting in front of you with my staff. Your work is to catch hold of the mind. Just close your eyes and go inside looking for it—find where it

of early morning at four o'clock, alone.... This man seems to be dangerous!" Bodhid harma always used to carry a big staff with him.

The emperor could not sleep the whole night, "To go or not to go? Because that man can do anything. He seems to be absolutely unpredictable." On the other hand, he felt deep down in his heart the sincerity of the man, that he was not a hypocrite. "He does not care a bit that you are an emperor and he is a beggar. He behaves as an emperor, and in front of him you are just a beggar. And the way he has said, 'I will put your mind at peace forever'....

is. The moment you catch hold of it, just tell me, 'Here it is.' And my staff will do the rest."

It was the strangest experience any seeker of truth or peace or silence could have ever had. But now there was no way out. Emperor Wu sat with closed eyes, knowing perfectly well that Bodhidharma seemed to mean what he said. He looked all around—there was no mind. That staff did its work!

For the first time he was in such a situation. The choice... if you find the mind, one never knows what this man is going to do with his staff. And in that silent mountainous place, in the presence of Bodhidharma, who has a charisma of his own....

There have been many enlightened people but Bodhidharma stands aloof, alone, like an Everest. His every act is unique and original. His every gesture has his own signature; it is not borrowed.

Emperor Wu tried hard to look for the mind and he could not find it. It is a small strategy. Mind exists only because you never look for it; it exists only because you are never aware of it.

When you are looking for it, you are aware of it, and awareness surely kills it completely. Hours passed and the sun was rising in the silent mountains with a cool breeze. Bodhidharma could see on the face of Emperor Wu such peace, such silence, such stillness... as if he were a statue. He shook him and asked him, "It has been a long time. Have you found the mind?"

Emperor Wu said, "Without using your staff, you have pacified my mind completely. I don't have any mind and I have heard the inner voice about which you spoke. Now I know that whatever you said was right. You have transformed me without doing anything. Now I know that each act has to be a reward unto itself; otherwise, don't do it. Who is there to give you the reward? This is a childish idea. Who is there to give you the punishment? Your action is punishment and your action is your reward. You are the master of your destiny."

Bodhidharma said, "You are a rare disciple. I love you. I respect you, not as an emperor, but as a man who has the courage just in a

single sitting to bring so much awareness, so much light that all darkness of the mind disappears."

Wu tried to persuade Bodhidharma to come to the palace. But Bodhidharma said, "That is not my place. You can see I am wild, I do things I myself don't know beforehand that I'm going to do. I live moment to moment, spontaneously. I am very unpredictable. I may create unnecessary trouble for you and your court, your people. I am not meant for palaces; just let me live in my wildness."

He lived on a mountain whose name was Tai. The second legend is that Bodhidharma was the man who created tea—the name *tea* comes from the mountain *Tai*, because it was created there. All the words for tea, in any language, are derived from the same source, *tai*.

The way Bodhidharma created tea cannot be historical, but it is significant. He was meditating almost all the time, and sometimes in the night he would start falling asleep. So, just to stay awake and teach a lesson to his eyes, he pulled out all his eyelashes and threw them on the temple ground. The story is that out of those eyelashes, the tea bushes grew. Those were the first tea bushes. That's why when you drink tea, you cannot sleep. Tea is immensely helpful during meditation. Today the Buddhist world drinks tea as part of meditation, because it keeps you alert and awake.

Although there were two million Buddhist monks in China, Bodhidharma could find only four who were worthy to be accepted as his disciples. He was so choosy, it took him almost nine years to find his first disciple, Hui-k'o.

For nine years—and that is a historical fact based on ancient references, almost contemporary to Bodhidharma which all mention that fact—for nine years, after sending Wu back to the palace, Bodhidharma sat facing a wall inside the temple. He made it a great meditation. He would simply look at the wall. After looking at a wall for a long time, you cannot think. Slowly, slowly, just like the wall, the screen of your mind also becomes empty. Bodhidharma had a second reason. He declared, "Unless somebody who deserves to be my disciple comes, I will not look at the audience."

People used to come and sit behind him. It was a strange situation. Nobody had spoken in this way before; he would speak to the wall. People would be sitting behind him but he would not face the audience because, he said, "The audience hurts me more, because it is just *like* a wall. Nobody understands, and to look at human beings in such an ignorant state hurts deeply. But to look at the wall, there is no question...a wall, after all, is a wall. It *cannot* hear, so there is no need to feel hurt. I will turn to face the audience only if somebody proves by his action that he is ready to be my disciple."

Nine years passed. People could not figure out what to do, what action would satisfy him. They could not figure it out. Then came a young man, Hui-k'o. He cut off one of his hands with a sword, threw the hand before Bodhidharma, and said, "This is the beginning. Either you turn, or my head will be falling before you. I am going to cut my head off too." Bodhidharma turned and said, "You are really a man worthy of me. No need to cut the head off; we have to use it." This man, Hui-k'o, was his first disciple. When Bodhidharma finally intended to leave China, he called his four disciples—three more he had gathered after Hui-k'o. He said to them, "In simple words, in small sentences, telegraphic, tell me the essence of my teachings. I intend to leave tomorrow morning to go back to the Himalayas, and I want to choose from you four, one as my successor."

The first man said, "Your teaching is of going beyond mind, of being absolutely silent, and then everything starts happening of its own accord."

Bodhidharma said, "You are not wrong, but you don't satisfy me. You just have my skin."

The second one said, "To know that I am not, and only existence is, is your fundamental teaching."

Bodhidharma said, "A little better, but not up to my standard. You have my bones; sit down."

And the third one said, "Nothing can be said about it. No word is capable of saying anything about it."

Bodhidharma said, "Good, but you have said already something about it. You have contradicted yourself. Just sit down; you have my marrow."

The fourth was his first disciple, Hui-k'o, who simply fell at Bodhidharma's feet, without saying a word, tears rolling down from his eyes. Bodhidharma said, "You have said it. You are going to be my successor."

But during the night, Bodhidharma was poisoned by some disciple out of revenge for not having been chosen as the successor. So they buried him, and the strangest legend is that after three years he was found by a government official, walking out of China toward the Himalayas with his staff in his hand, and one of his sandals hanging from the staff—and he was barefoot. The official had known him, had been to see him many times, had fallen in love with the man, although he was a little eccentric. He asked, "What is the meaning of this staff, and one sandal hanging from it?" Bodhidharma said, "Soon you will know. If you meet my people just tell them that I'm going into the Himalayas forever."

The official rushed immediately, as fast as he could, to the monastery on the mountain where Bodhidharma had been living. There he heard that Bodhidharma had been poisoned and had died...and there was the tomb. The official had not heard about it because he was posted on the boundary of the empire. He said, "My God, but I have seen him, and I cannot be deceived because I have seen him many times before. He was the same man, those same ferocious eyes, the same fiery and wild outlook, and on top of it, he was carrying one sandal on his staff."

The disciples could not contain their curiosity, and they opened the tomb. All they found there was just one sandal. And then the official understood why he had said, "Soon you will know."

We have heard so much about Jesus' resurrection. But nobody has talked much of the resurrection of Bodhidharma. Perhaps he was only in a coma when they buried him, and then he came to his senses, slipped out of the tomb, left one sandal there and put another sandal on his staff and according to the plan, he left.

He wanted to die in the eternal snows of the Himalayas. He wanted there to be no tomb, no temple, no statue of him. He did not want to leave any footprints behind him to be worshiped; those who loved him should enter into their own being. "I am not going to be worshiped," he said. And he disappeared almost in thin air. Nobody heard anything more about him—what happened, where he died. He must be buried in the eternal snows of the Himalayas.

a marriage
with tao

Zen is a crossbreed between Buddha's thought and Lao Tzu's thought. It is a great meeting, the greatest that ever took place.

sosan, the third zen patriarch

Zen goes beyond Buddha and beyond Lao Tzu. It is a culmination, a transcendence, both of the Indian genius and of the Chinese genius. The Indian genius reached its highest peak in Gautam the Buddha and the Chinese genius reached its highest peak in Lao Tzu. And the meeting between the essence of Buddha's teaching and the essence of Lao Tzu's teaching merged into one stream so deeply that no separation is possible now. Even to make a distinction between what belongs to Buddha and what to Lao Tzu is impossible, the merger has been so total. It is not only a synthesis, it is an integration. Out of this meeting Zen was born. Zen is neither Buddhist nor Taoist and yet it is both.

SOSAN IS THE third Zen Patriarch. Nothing much is known about him, and this is as it should be because history records only violence. History does not record silence—it cannot record it. All records are of disturbance. Whenever someone becomes truly silent, he disappears from all records; he is no longer a part of our madness. So it is as it should be.

Sosan remained a wandering monk his whole life. He never stayed anywhere; he was always passing by, going along, moving. He was a river; he was not a pond, static. He was a constant movement. That is the meaning of Buddha calling his monks *bhikkhus,* "wanderers": not only in the outside world, but also in the inside world they should be homeless, because whenever you make a home you become attached to it. They should

remain rootless; there is no home for them apart from this whole universe.

Even when it was recognized that Sosan had become enlightened, he continued his old beggar's way. Nothing was special about him. He was an ordinary man, a man of Tao.

One thing I would like to remind you of: Zen is a crossbreed. And just as more beautiful flowers can come out of crossbreeding, and more beautiful children are born out of crossbreeding, the same has happened with Zen.

Zen is a crossbreed between Buddha's thought and Lao Tzu's thought. It is a great meeting, the greatest that ever took place. That's why Zen is more beautiful than Buddha's thought and more beautiful than Lao Tzu's thought. It is a rare flowering of

the highest peaks and the meeting of those peaks. Zen is neither Buddhist nor Taoist, but it carries both within it.

India is a little too serious about religion—there is a long past, a great weight on the mind of India, and religion has become serious. Lao Tzu remained a laughingstock—he is known as the old fool. He is not serious at all; you cannot find a more non-serious man. When Buddha's thought and Lao Tzu's thought met, India and China met, and Zen was born. Sosan was near the original source when Zen was coming out of the womb. He carries the fundamentals.

His biography is not relevant at all, because whenever a man becomes enlightened he has no biography. He is no longer confined to his form, so when he was born and when he died are irrelevant facts.

That's why in the East we have never bothered about biographies, about historical facts. That obsession has never existed in the East. That obsession has come from the West only recently, now that people have become more interested in irrelevant things.

When a Sosan is born, what difference does it make—this year or that? When he dies, how is it important? Sosan is important, not his entry into this world and the body, not his departure. Arrivals and departures are irrelevant. The only relevance is in the being.

In his lifetime, Sosan only uttered a few words. Remember, they are not just words, because they come out of a mind that has gone beyond words. They are not speculations; they are authentic experiences. Whatsoever he says, he knows. He is not a man of knowledge; he is a wise man. He has penetrated the mystery and whatever he brings forth is significant. It can transform you completely. If you listen to him, the very listening can become a transformation, because whatsoever he is saying is the purest gold.

When Sosan speaks, he speaks on a different plane. He is not interested in speaking; he is not interested in influencing anybody; he is not trying to convince you of some theory or philosophy or ism. No, when he speaks, his silence blooms. When he speaks, he is saying that which he has come to know and would like to share with you. It is not to convince you, remember—it is just to share with you. If you can understand a single word

of his, you will feel a tremendous silence being released within you.

We will be talking about Sosan and his words. If you listen attentively, suddenly you will feel a release of silence within you. These words are atomic, they are full of energy. Whenever a person who has attained says something, the word is a seed and for millions of years the word will remain a seed and will seek a heart.

If you are ready, ready to become the soil, then these tremendously powerful words of Sosan—these living seeds—will enter your heart if you allow it, and you will be totally different through them. Don't listen to them from the mind, because their meaning is not of the mind; the mind is absolutely impotent to understand them. They don't come from the mind, they cannot be understood by the mind. They come from a no-mind. They can be understood only by a state of no-mind.

So while listening, don't try to interpret. Don't listen to the words but to the gaps between the lines, not to what he says but to what he means—the significance. Let that significance hover around you like a fragrance. Silently it will enter you; you will become pregnant. But don't interpret. Don't say, "He means this or that," because that interpretation will be yours. Don't interpret—listen. When you interpret you can't listen, because the consciousness cannot do two opposite things simultaneously. If you start thinking, listening stops. Just listen as you listen to music—a different quality of listening in which there is no meaning in the sounds.

This is also music. This Sosan is a musician, not a philosopher. This Sosan is not saying words, he is saying more—more than the words. They have significance but they don't have any meaning. They are like musical sounds.

When you sit near a waterfall, you listen to it, but do you interpret what the waterfall says? It says nothing, yet it speaks. It says much that cannot be said.

What do you do near a waterfall? You listen, you become silent and quiet, you absorb. You allow the waterfall to go deeper and deeper within you. Then everything becomes quiet and silent within. You become a temple—the unknown enters through the waterfall.

What do you do when you listen to the songs of the birds, or wind passing through the trees, or dry leaves being blown by the breeze? What do you do? You simply listen.

This Sosan is not a philosopher, he is not a theologian, he is not a priest. He does not want to sell any idea to you, he is not interested in ideas. He is not there to convince you, he is simply blooming. He is a waterfall, or he is a wind blowing through the trees, or he is a song of the birds—no meaning, but much significance. You have to absorb that significance, only then will you be able to understand.

So listen, but don't think. Then it will be possible for much to happen within you, because I tell you: this Sosan, about whom nothing much is known, was a man of power, a man who has come to know. When he speaks he carries something of the unknown to the world of the known. With him enters the divine, a ray of light into the darkness of your mind.

Before we enter into his words, remember the significance of the words, not the meaning; the music, the melody, not the meaning; the sound of his soundless mind, his heart, not his thinking. You have to listen to his being, the waterfall.

How to listen? Just be silent. Don't bring your mind in. Don't start thinking, "What is he saying?" Just listen without deciding this way or that, without saying whether he is right or wrong, whether you are convinced or not. He does not bother about your conviction; you also need not bother about it. Simply listen and delight. Such persons as Sosan are to be delighted in; they are natural phenomena.

A beautiful rock—what do you do with it? You delight in it. You touch it, you move around it, you feel it, the moss on it.

What do you do with clouds moving in the sky? You dance on the earth, you look at them, or you just keep quiet and lie down on the ground and watch them float.

And they fill you. Not only the outer sky— by and by, the more you become silent, they fill your inner sky also.

Suddenly you are not there; only clouds are moving, in and out. The division is dropped, the boundary is no more. You have become the sky and the sky has become you.

Treat Sosan as a natural phenomenon. He is not just a man, he is godliness, he is Tao, he is a buddha. This Sosan is not for logic, he is for life. Now, try to understand the significance of his words. He says:

The Great Way is not difficult for those who have no preferences.

When love and hate are both absent everything becomes clear and undisguised.

Make the smallest distinction, however, and heaven and earth are set infinitely apart.

If you wish to see the truth, then hold no opinion for or against.

The struggle of what one likes and what one dislikes is the disease of the mind.

Just as Chuang Tzu says, "Easy is right," Sosan says, "The Great Way is not difficult." If it appears difficult, it is you who make it difficult. The Great Way is easy. How can it be difficult? Even trees follow it, rivers follow it, rocks follow it. How can it be difficult? Even birds fly in it and fish swim in it. How can it be difficult? People make it difficult, the mind makes it difficult—and the trick to make any easy thing difficult is to choose, to make a distinction.

Love is easy, hate is easy, yet you choose. You say, "I will only love, I will not hate." Now everything has become difficult. Now you cannot even love! To breathe in is easy, to breathe out is easy. You choose. You say, "I will only breathe in, I will not breathe out." Now everything has become difficult.

The mind can ask, "Why breathe out? Breath is life. Simple arithmetic: go on breathing in, don't breathe out, and you will become more and more alive. More and more life will be accumulated. You will become a great treasure of life. Breathe in only; don't breathe out because breathing out is death."

Remember, the first thing a child has to do when he is born is to breathe in. And the last thing a man does when he dies is to breathe out. Life begins with breathing in and death begins with breathing out. Each moment when you breathe in you are reborn; each moment when you breathe out you are dead, because breath is life. That's why Hindus have called it *prana*: *prana* means life. Breath is life.

The simple logic, simple arithmetic; there is not much trouble, you can make it plain: more and more breathe in and don't breathe out, then you will never die. If you breathe out you will have to die. And if you do it too much you will die soon! Simple arithmetic, it seems so obvious. So what is a logician supposed to do? A logician will only breathe in, never breathe out.

Love is breathing in, hate is breathing out. So what to do? Life is easy if you don't decide, because then you know breathing in and breathing out are not two opposite things; they are two parts of one process. Those two parts are organically connected, you cannot divide them. And if you don't breathe out…? The logic is wrong. You will not be alive—you will be simply, immediately, dead.

Try it—just breathe in and don't breathe out. You will understand. You will become very, very tense. Your whole being would like to breathe out because this is leading to death. If you choose, you will be in difficulty. If you don't choose, everything is easy. Easy is right.

If you are in difficulty, it is because of too many teachers who have poisoned your mind, who have been teaching you: "Choose this—don't do this, do that." Their dos and don'ts have killed you, yet they look logical. If you argue with them they will win the argument. Logic will help them: "Look! It is so simple. Why breathe out if it brings death?"

The same thing has happened with sex, in some traditions, because people think death enters with sex. They seem to be right, because sex energy gives birth to life, so the more sex energy moves out, the more life is moving out. It is logical, absolutely Aristotelian, but foolish. You cannot find greater fools than logicians. It is logical that life energy comes from sex—a child is born because of sex, sex is the source of life—so keep it in. Don't allow it to go out, otherwise you will be dead. Thus the world has become afraid.

But this is the same as keeping the breath in; if you suppress it, the whole being wants to throw it out. So your so-called celibates, who try to keep their sex energy in, find that the whole body wants to throw that energy out.

Their entire lives become sexual—their minds become sexual, they dream of sex, they think of sex all the time. Sex becomes their obsession because they are trying to do something that is logical, of course, but not true to life.

If you want more life, breathe out more, so you create a vacuum inside and more breath comes in. Don't think about breathing in, simply exhale as much as you can and your whole being will inhale. Love more—that is breathing out—and your body will gather energy from the whole cosmos. You create the vacuum and the energy comes.

It is like this in every process of life. You eat, but then you become a miser, you become constipated. The logic is right: don't breathe out. Constipation is choosing to breathe in and being against breathing out. Almost every civilized person is constipated; you can measure civilization through constipation. The more constipated a country the more civilized because the more logical. Why breathe out? Just go on breathing in. Food is energy. Why throw it out? You may not be aware of it, but this is the unconscious mind being logical and Aristotelian.

Life is a balance between throwing out and inviting in. You are just a passage. Share! Give, and more will be given to you. Be a miser, don't give, and less will be given to you because you don't need it.

Remember, and watch your life processes. If you are interested in understanding enlightenment ultimately, remember to give so that more is given to you, whatsoever it is.

Breathe out, exhale more. That is what sharing means, what giving means.

But the mind has its own logic, and Sosan calls that logic the disease.

The Great Way is not difficult... You make it difficult, *you* are difficult. The Great Way is easy...*for those who have no preferences.*

Don't prefer—just allow life to move. Don't say to life, "Move this way, go to the north, or go to the south." Don't say anything; simply flow with life. Don't fight against the current; become one with the current.

The Great Way is easy for those who have no preferences, and you have preferences about everything! About everything you bring in your mind. You say, "I like, I don't like, I prefer this, I don't prefer that." But when you have no preferences—when all 'for' and 'against' attitudes are absent, both love and hate are absent, you have neither likes nor dislikes—you simply allow everything to happen. Then, Sosan says, "Everything becomes clear and undisguised."

Make the smallest distinction, however, and heaven and earth are set infinitely apart.

But your mind will say, "You will become an animal if you don't prefer. If you don't choose then what will be the difference between you and a tree?" There will be a difference, a great difference—not a difference that brings the mind in but a difference that comes through awareness. The tree is choiceless and unconscious. You will be choiceless and *conscious*. That is what choiceless awareness means, and that is the greatest distinction: you will be *aware that you are not choosing*.

This awareness gives such profound peace...you become a buddha, you become a Sosan, a Chuang Tzu. The tree cannot become a Chuang Tzu. Chuang Tzu is like the tree, and something more. He is like the tree as far as choice is concerned, he is absolutely unlike the tree as far as awareness is concerned. He is fully aware that he is not choosing.

Sosan says: *When love and hate are both absent....*

Love and hate both color your sight and then you cannot see clearly. If you love a person, you start seeing things that are not there. No woman is as beautiful as you think she is when you love her, because you project. You have a dream girl in mind and that dream girl is projected. Somehow the real girl functions only as a screen. That's why every love comes to frustration sooner or later, because how can the girl go on playing the screen? She is a real person; she will assert herself, she will say, "I am not a screen!" How long can she go on fitting in with your projection? Sooner or later you feel the projection doesn't fit. In the beginning she yielded to you, in the beginning you yielded to her. You were a projection screen for her, and she was a projection screen for you.

Mulla Nasruddin's wife said to him, "You don't love me as much as you loved me before, when you were courting me."

Nasruddin said, "Darling, don't pay much attention to those things—it was just campaign propaganda. I'll forget what you said if you forget what I said. Now let's get real."

> *Drop all burdens.*
>
> *The higher you want to reach,*
>
> *the less burdened you must be*

Nobody can play a screen for you forever because it is uncomfortable. How can somebody adjust to your dream? He has his own reality, and that reality asserts itself.

If you love a person, you project things that are not there. If you hate a person, again you project things that are not there. In love the person becomes a god, in hate the person becomes a devil—and the person is neither a god nor a devil, the person is simply himself or herself. These devils and gods are projections. If you love, you cannot see clearly. If you hate, you cannot see clearly.

When there is no liking and no disliking, your eyes are clear; you have clarity. Then you see the other as he is or she is. When you have a clarity of consciousness the whole existence reveals its reality to you. That reality is divine, that reality is truth.

What does it mean? Does it mean that a man like Sosan will not love? No, but his love will have a totally different quality; it will not be like yours. He will love but his love will not be a choice. He will love but his love will not be a projection. He will love but his love will not be a love for his own dream. He will love the real.

That love toward the real is compassion. He will not project this way or that. He will not see a god in you or a devil. He will simply see you. And he will share because he has enough— and the more one shares, the more it grows. He will share his ecstasy with you.

When you love, you project. You love not to give, you love to take, you love to exploit. When you love a person you start trying to fix the person according to your ideas. Every husband is doing that, every wife is doing that, every friend. They go on trying to change the other, the real—and since the real cannot be changed, they will only get frustrated. The real cannot be changed, so only your dream will be shattered and you will feel hurt. You don't listen to reality.

Nobody is here to fulfill your dream. Everybody is here to fulfill his own destiny, his own reality.

A man like Sosan loves but his love is not an exploitation. He loves because he has so much that he is overflowing. He is not creating a dream around anybody. He shares with whoever comes on his path. His sharing is unconditional, and he does not expect a thing from you.

If love expects anything, then there will be frustration. If love expects something, then there will be unfulfillment. If love expects something, there is going to be misery and madness.

"No," says Sosan, "neither love nor hate. Simply look at the reality of the other." This is Buddha's love: to see the reality of the other— not to project, not to dream, not to create an

image, not to try to fix the other according to your image.

Sosan says: *"When love and hate are both absent, everything becomes clear and undisguised."*

Mind has to love and hate, and mind has to go on fighting between these two. If you don't love and don't hate, you go beyond mind. Where is the mind then? When choice disappears within you, the mind disappears.

But even if you say, "I would like to be silent," you will never be silent because you have a preference. This is the problem.

People say, "I would like to be silent. I don't want these tensions anymore." I feel sorry for them—sorry because what they are saying is stupid. If you "don't want tensions anymore"

you will create new ones, because not-wanting is going to create a new tension. If you want silence too much, if you are striving for it too much, your silence itself will become a tension. Now you will be more disturbed because of your effort to catch hold of silence.

What is silence? It is a deep understanding of the phenomenon that if you prefer, you will be tense. Even if you prefer silence, you will be tense. Understand, feel it—whenever you prefer, you become tense; whenever you don't prefer, there is no tension and you are relaxed. When you are relaxed, your eyes have clarity; they are not crowded with clouds and dreams. No thoughts move in the mind; you can see the true. And when you can see the true, you are liberated. Truth liberates.

"Make the smallest distinction, however, and heaven and earth are set infinitely apart," says Sosan. The smallest distinction, the slightest choice, and you are divided. Then you have a hell and a heaven, and between these two you will be crushed.

"If you wish to see the truth, then hold no opinion for or against," says Sosan. Move without opinion. Move naked, with no clothes, with no opinions about truth, because truth abhors all opinions. Drop all your philosophies, theories, doctrines, scriptures! Drop all rubbish! Become silent, unchoosing, your eyes ready to see what is, not in any way hoping to see your wishes fulfilled.

Don't carry wishes. It is said the path to hell is completely filled with wishes—good wishes, hopes, dreams, rainbows, ideals. The path to heaven is absolutely empty.

Drop all burdens. The higher you want to reach, the less burdened you must be. If you go to the Himalayas you have to unburden yourself completely. Finally, when you reach the Gourishankar, the Everest, you have to drop everything.

You have to go completely naked, because the higher you move the more weightless you need to be. And opinions are weights on you. They are not wings, they are like paperweights. Be opinionless, without any preference... "If you wish to see the truth then hold no opinion for or against."

Don't be a theist and don't be an atheist if you really want to know what truth is. Don't say, "There is a God" and don't say, "There is no God," because whatever you say will become a deep desire and you will project whatever is hidden in the desire.

If you want to see God as a Krishna with a flute on his lips, someday you will see him— not because Krishna is there, only because you had a seed of desire that you projected on the screen of the world. If you want to see Jesus crucified, you will see that. Whatsoever you want will be projected, but it is just a dream world—you are not coming nearer to the truth.

Become seedless within: no opinion, no thought for or against, no philosophy. Simply go to see that which is. Don't carry any mind. Go mindless.

"If you wish to see the truth then hold no opinion for or against. The struggle of what one likes and what one dislikes is the disease of the mind."

This is the disease of the mind: what one likes and what one does not like, for and against. Why is the mind divided? Why can't you be one? You would like to be one, you want to be one, but you go on watering the divisions, the preferences, the likes and dislikes. The more you use the mind, the more it is strengthened, the stronger it becomes. Don't use it.

Difficult, because you will say, "What will happen to our love? What will happen to our belonging? What will happen to our beliefs? What will happen to our religion, church, and temple?" They are your burdens. Be freed of them, and let them be freed of you. They are keeping you here, rooted, and truth would want you to be liberated.

Liberated you reach, with wings you reach, weightless you reach.

Says Sosan: "The struggle of what one likes and what one dislikes is the disease of the mind."

How to overcome it? Is there any way to overcome it? No, there is no way. One has simply to understand it. One has simply to look at the facticity of it. One has just to close one's eyes and look at one's own life—watch it, and you will feel the truth of Sosan. And when you feel the truth, the disease drops. There is no medicine for it because if medicine is given to you, you will start liking the medicine. Then the disease will be forgotten but the medicine will be liked, and then the medicine becomes a disease.

No, Sosan is not going to give you any medicine, any method. He is not going to suggest what to do. He is simply going to insist again and again and again, a thousand and one times, that you understand how you have created this mess around you, how you are in such misery. Nobody else has created it; it is your mind's disease of preference, of choosing.

Don't choose. Accept life as it is in its totality. You must look at the total: life and death together, love and hate together, happiness and unhappiness together, agony and ecstasy together.

If you look at them together, then what is there to choose? If you see they are one, then from where can choice enter? If you see that agony is nothing but ecstasy, ecstasy nothing but agony; if you can see that happiness is nothing but unhappiness; love is nothing but hate, hate is nothing but love—then where to choose? How to choose?

Then choice drops. *You* are not dropping it. If *you* drop it, that will become a choice—this is the paradox. You are not supposed to drop it, because if you drop it that means you have chosen for and against.

Now your choice is for totality. You are for totality and against division, but the disease has entered. It is subtle.

Simply understand, and the very understanding becomes dropping. Never drop it. Simply laugh... and ask for a cup of tea.

PLATE NUMBER ONE

PLATE NUMBER TWO

TENDING THE OX—A ZEN ALLEGORY

Tending the ox is an ancient symbol in the history of Zen. There exist ten paintings in China; the tenth painting has been a cause of great controversy. I would like you to understand those ten paintings.

The ten paintings are immensely beautiful. In the first, the ox is lost. The man to whom the ox belongs is standing, looking all around in the thick forest, and he cannot see where the ox has gone. He is simply bewildered, confused. It is getting late, the sun it setting; soon it will be night, and then going into the thick forest to find the ox will become more and more difficult.

In the second picture he finds hoofprints of the ox. He feels a little happier; perhaps there is a possibility of finding the ox—he has found the hoofprints. He follows them.

In the third picture he sees the back of the ox standing in the thick forest. It is difficult to see, but he can figure out that it is the back of his ox. In the fourth he has reached the ox; he can see the ox now, its whole body. He rejoices.

In the fifth painting he takes hold of the ox's horns. It is a great struggle to bring it back home, but he wins. In the sixth picture he is riding on the ox, coming back toward his home. These are beautiful paintings!

In the seventh picture the ox is tied down in his place. In the eighth picture the man is so full of joy that he starts playing on his flute. The ninth picture is an empty frame—there is nothing painted in it.

In the tenth picture, which is the cause of a great controversy, the man is going with a bottle of wine toward the marketplace, almost drunk. You can see, he cannot even walk. This tenth picture has caused a great controversy which has been raging for two thousand years.

One sect, which is the major sect of mahayana, believes that the ninth is the last picture. It represents the no-mind; you have achieved the goal. The ox is your innermost self which you have lost, and the whole series of pictures is in search of your inner self. You have found the self in the ninth. There is immense silence and peace. It is nirvana; it is no-mind.

Beyond the ninth... the people who say this is the end of the journey think that somebody has added the tenth picture, which seems to be absolutely irrelevant. But the people who belong to a certain small sect of Zen believe in the tenth picture, too. They say that when one has become enlightened this is not the end. This is the highest peak of consciousness, it is the greatest achievement, but one has to come back to the human world, to the ordinary world. One has to again become part of the greater humanity. Only then can he share, only then can he provoke others to the search. And certainly when he comes from such height, he is absolutely drunk with ecstasy. That bottle of wine is not an ordinary wine. It is symbolic of an ecstatic state.

When these pictures were brought to Japan, just twelve or thirteen hundred years ago, only

PLATE NUMBER THREE

PLATE NUMBER FOUR

nine pictures were brought. The tenth was troublesome; it was left in China.

I was puzzled when I first looked at the Japanese pictures. They seem to be complete. Once you have achieved nirvana, what more is there? And then I found in an old Chinese book ten pictures. I was immensely happy that somebody had the insight two thousand years ago that a buddha is not a buddha if he cannot come back to ordinary humanity, if he cannot again become simple, innocent, carrying his nirvana, carrying his ecstasy in the bottle of wine, utterly drunk with the divine but still going toward the marketplace.

I could see that whoever painted the tenth picture was right. Up to the ninth picture, it is simply logical. Beyond the ninth, the tenth is a great realization.

PLATE NUMBER FIVE

According to me, up to the ninth a man is only a buddha; with the tenth he also becomes a Zorba. And this has been my constant theme: I have been insisting that the tenth picture is authentic, and if it were not there, I was going to paint it. Without it, ending in nothingness looks a little sad, looks a little serious, looks empty.

All this effort of finding yourself, meditating, going beyond the mind, realizing your being and ending up in desert of nothingness...no, there must be something more to it, something more beyond it, where flowers blossom, where songs arise, where dance is again possible—of course, on a totally different level.

These pictures of tending the ox have been found to be tremendously significant in explaining the whole path step by step.

PLATE NUMBER SIX

PLATE NUMBER SEVEN

PLATE NUMBER NINE

PLATE NUMBER EIGHT

PLATE NUMBER TEN

rinzai, master of the
irrational

Rinzai became known as "the master of shouts."

He used shouting as a method to bring silence to people.

z e n   g o e s   t o   j a p a n

Rinzai was one of the loveliest masters in the history of Zen. He brought Zen from China to Japan, but he had lived with the Chinese masters. He carried the same flame that Bodhidharma took from India to China. He had something of the same greatness, beauty, and the same absurd approach to awakening.

R INZAI IS ONE of the most loved masters in the tradition of Zen. The first transmission of the light happened between Gautam Buddha and Mahakashyapa. The second great transmission happened between Bodhidharma and his successor, Hui-k'o. Bodhidharma took the ultimate experience of consciousness from India to China.

Rinzai introduced the same consciousness, the same path of entering into oneself, from China to Japan. These three names—Mahakashyapa, Bodhidharma, and Rinzai—stand like great peaks of the Himalayas.

Rinzai became known as "the master of shouts." He used shouting as a method to bring silence to people—a sudden shout. They are asking about God, they are asking about heaven, they are asking about great philosophical or theological problems…and the master suddenly shouts!

The mind gets a shock, almost an electric shock. For a moment you are not, only the shout is. For a moment the mind stops, time stops—and that is the secret of meditation.

Rinzai would shout at the disciples to give them a first experience of their centering. You are both a circumference and a center. You live on the circumference; the shout pushes you to the center.

Once you experience being at the center you suddenly see the whole world changing. Your eyes are no longer the same; your clarity and transparency are absolute. You see the same green leaves greener, the same roses rosier, the same life as a festival, as a ceremony. You would love to dance.

Then the disciples learned that the shout could help them reach to their very center. It was a strange sight when Rinzai started accepting disciples near the river. The disciples

> **" Once you experience being at the center, you suddenly see the whole world changing "**

  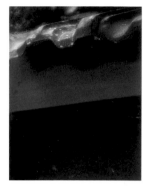

would be shouting and the valley would resound with shouts.

You could tell from miles away that you were getting closer to Rinzai. It was not only that he was shouting, but that shouting was a method to throw you from the circumference to the center.

Many mystics around the world have used sounds, but usually in a superficial way. Rinzai used shouts in a tremendously deep way. His shouts would become like a sword entering into you, piercing to the very center.

Another example is Jalaluddin Rumi's technique of whirling to find the center. If you whirl for hours, you will see slowly that something at the very center is not moving at all, and that is you. Your body is whirling, but your consciousness is a pillar of light.

Rumi attained his first enlightenment by whirling for thirty-six hours continuously. People thought he was mad. Even today a small group of his followers continues. They are called whirling dervishes. But the point is the same: whirling, your body becomes a cyclone, and your witnessing self becomes the center. Everything moves around you, but the center remains unmoving. To know this unmoving center is to know the master key of all the mysteries of life.

Rinzai had no idea about Rumi, neither did Rumi have any idea about Rinzai, but both were working on the same strategy—how to get to the center. As your consciousness becomes deeper, as it becomes an easy thing to go to the center just like you go into your house and come out again, you have become a buddha. Then slowly, slowly your center starts changing your circumference. First you cannot be violent; then you cannot be destructive; then you are love. Not that you love—you *are* love. Then you are silence, then you are truth, all that is old in you has disappeared. That was your circumference, that was the cyclone, and now it is gone. Now, only the center remains.

Rinzai said:

If you meet a buddha, cut him down; if you meet a patriarch, cut him down; if you meet an

arhat, cut him down; if you meet your parents, cut them down; and if you meet your relatives, cut them down.

Only thus will you be liberated, and if you are not held by externals, you will be disengaged and comfortably independent.

After this mountain monk has said that there is no dharma externally, students who do not understand this immediately make their interpretation of the internal. They then sit against the wall with the tongue touching the palate, to be in a motionless position and regard this as the Buddha Dharma of the patriarchs.

The greatest mistake is that if you take immobility as the right state, you will mistake the darkness for your master. This is what an ancient meant when he said, "In complete darkness, an abyss is dreadful."

If you take the moving state as the right one, all plants and straws can move. Are they Tao? Therefore, the moving is the element wind, and the unmoving is the element earth. Both the moving and the unmoving have no nature of their own. If you want to catch it in the moving, it will go to the unmoving; and if you want to catch it in the unmoving, it will go to the moving.

The moving and unmoving are two kinds of states, but the man of Tao can make use of both.

One of the fundamentals of Zen that makes it a unique religion, like no other religion in the world, is that it does not want to exclude anything from your life. Your life has to be all-inclusive; it has to comprehend all the stars and the sky and the earth. Zen is not a path of renouncing the world.

People are taught to sit silently with their tongue touching their palate, so even inside their mouth they cannot make any movement of the tongue, and the whole body should be like a statue—only then can you realize the truth. But it is only half of the truth, and a half truth is more dangerous than a total lie; at least a lie is total.

Life is both rest and movement.

If you go to Bodhgaya, where Gautam Buddha became enlightened, there stands a temple in memory of his enlightenment, by the side of the tree where he used to sit and meditate. That was his routine: for one hour he would sit under the tree and meditate, then for one hour he would walk by the side of the tree. Even the places where he moved are marked by stones to reveal a small path.

One hour he would walk and meditate, showing perfectly that life, if it is unmoving, is dead. And life, if it has no rest, will end very soon.

Life is a balance between rest and movement. When harmony is achieved between rest and movement, you come to the very center of your life, which is always with you whether you are sitting or moving, whether you are awake or asleep. Its existence is absolutely certain, but not discovered by reading scriptures. You have to experience it, then you can do anything. Then there is no problem for you, because whatever you do will be done out of a buddha nature.

The meditation that Buddha gave to the world is perhaps one of the most significant. There are many meditations, many ways to enter into yourself, but Buddha's is sharp, almost like a sword—it cuts everything that hinders. Even in a split second, you can reach to your ultimate destiny. But for that, Rinzai says: "If you meet a buddha...." He does not mean the actual Buddha, because where will you meet him now? Even when Rinzai was alive, Buddha had been dead for almost fifteen hundred years. So what is the meaning?

"If you meet a buddha, cut him down...."

It is a meditation process. When you go deeper into yourself, you are bound to meet figures who are very close to your heart. If you have loved Buddha, you are going to meet Buddha before you meet yourself. It will be just an image, but in the silences of the heart that image will be so radiant that there is a possibility you may sit down at the side of the road with of the image and forget that this is not the goal.

"If you meet a buddha, cut him down"—immediately! "If you meet a patriarch, a master, cut him down"—immediately! "If you meet an arhat, cut him down; if you meet your parents, cut them down; and if you meet your relatives, cut them down. Only thus will you be liberated...."

It is an inner psychological process, making you free from the master, from the parents, from the friends. It has nothing to do with the outside world, it is your inner world where images go on gathering. And unless all these images are dissolved, you cannot see yourself. They are hindering your perception. Rinzai's description of the Buddhist meditation is excellent.

"And if you are not held by externals, you will be disengaged and comfortably independent."

Now you have destroyed all the images, your dreams, your love affairs. You have made the path clean, but you may still be attached to externals. You may be ready to cut away your parents' image and be free of it, but what of the desire for power in the world, the desire to be the richest man in the world? A thousand and one desires surround you in the external world. The second step is easier. Rinzai begins with the hardest because he knows if you can do the hardest, the easier can be done without any difficulty.

"After this mountain monk has said that there is no dharma externally, students who do not understand this immediately make their interpretation of the internal."

It is very easy to misunderstand a master. In fact, it is easier to misunderstand a master than anyone else, because he is speaking a new language, giving new meanings to words, talking about spaces you have never been to. It is human to be mistaken, to misunderstand.

He says: "After this mountain monk has said that there is no dharma externally...." There is no religion externally. Going to the temple or to the church or to the synagogue, reading scriptures, ancient holy books—these are all externals and there is no dharma as far as externals are concerned. They are dead skeletons, remnants of somebody who attained, but now it is too difficult to decode the scriptures. The man is no longer there—only the skeleton of the man, which cannot speak, which cannot explain, which cannot help you in any way.

You can go on carrying scriptures, but those scriptures will be your interpretations, not the meaning of the masters.

You can go to the temples outside, but what are you doing? Going to manmade temples, full of manmade gods, and you are worshipping those stone gods. And you are not alone; almost the whole world is worshipping something or other as a god. But in this way you cannot find the essence of dharma. It is a very upside down, disturbed, and perverted situation when man starts worshipping gods he has created himself.

You have to know the source of life—the source from which you spring, just as roses spring. It is not a question of prayer, it is a question of intense exploration inside to find your roots. You will be surprised: your roots are the roots of the moon, of the sun, of the stars—of all existence.

You are just a small branch of a vast tree. Once you know it, there is no fear of death. You cannot die—you belong to immortality. There is no more desire. What more can you have? You have the whole universe in your hands. You are already everything you could have dreamed, desired, asked to be. A great contentment descends over you. In this contentment are all the qualities of blissfulness, of ecstasy, of all that is a continuous dance, a festivity, a ceremony.

Rinzai says, "But I can be misunderstood. When I say there is no dharma externally, people might then sit against the wall with the tongue touching the palate, to be in a motionless position and regard this as the buddha dharma of the patriarchs."

Just sitting…how long can you go on sitting? When you stand up, Bodhidharma or Buddha or Rinzai will say, "What happened to the buddha?" The Buddha was sitting; your form of the buddha experience was sitting, but when you stand it will disappear. Walking, you will be walking away from sitting.

Rinzai is trying to say things in simple terms, and he had to be very simple because he was the man who brought Zen from China to Japan. He was talking to absolutely unconcerned people who had never heard about meditation.

"The greatest mistake is that if you take immobility as the right state, you will mistake the darkness for your master."

Immobility is only a rest period. Existence is motion, continuous motion. Yes, there are moments of rest, but if you choose the moments of rest as the whole truth, you are accepting darkness as your master. You are cutting life in two: darkness and light. Have you watched one thing? Darkness is stable. It never goes anywhere, it is always here. You bring light and you cannot see darkness. You take the light away and darkness is already there. It does not come running in from the street; it is never late, not even a single moment. If it had gone out for an evening walk, or to have a look at what was happening around the world, there would be a gap. When you had taken the lights away, the darkness would not be there yet. But there is never a gap. The reason is that darkness is always here even when light is here; it is just because of the light that you cannot see the darkness. Even in the motion, the action, the gesture of a buddha, there is a certain restfulness. That restfulness brings a grace to it, a beauty to it.

Rinzai says: "This is what an ancient meant when he said, 'In complete darkness, an abyss is dreadful.'"

Meditation is not meant to divide your life and your existence in two parts and then to choose one, the internal. A perfect meditation is all-inclusive. It transforms you, and with your transformation your vision of things is transformed, but nothing is excluded.

If you take the moving state as the right one, all plants and straws can move. Are they Tao? Therefore, the moving is the element wind, and the unmoving is the element earth, and both the moving and the unmoving have no nature of their own. If you want to catch it in the moving, it will go to the unmoving....

They are continuously changing places: day becoming night, night becoming day; life becoming death, death becoming life. Don't hold onto anything. It will immediately change into something else.

The movement and the non-movement are both in your hands. You are the watcher, neither the moving nor the unmoving.

You simply are.

You have never moved, so the question of unmoving does not arise. The question of movement or no movement is irrelevant to your witnessing consciousness. Your witnessing consciousness is existential. It is here. If your meditation does not bring you to this state of watchfulness, it is a false meditation. If it brings you to any god, you are fooling yourself; you are dreaming. If it brings you to Jesus Christ, then... Jesus Christ! Rinzai is saying if you meet Jesus Christ, give him another cross immediately! "That is your work, what else are you all doing here?" Even Buddha is not spared—and they are all disciples of Buddha.

If you meet the Buddha on the way, cut his head immediately. Nothing is more important than your own internal watchfulness. That is the very stuff the universe is made of.

flowers
bloom

Anything can be used to find the truth. Even a warrior can use his sword, fighting with another warrior; there is no need for him to sit and meditate.

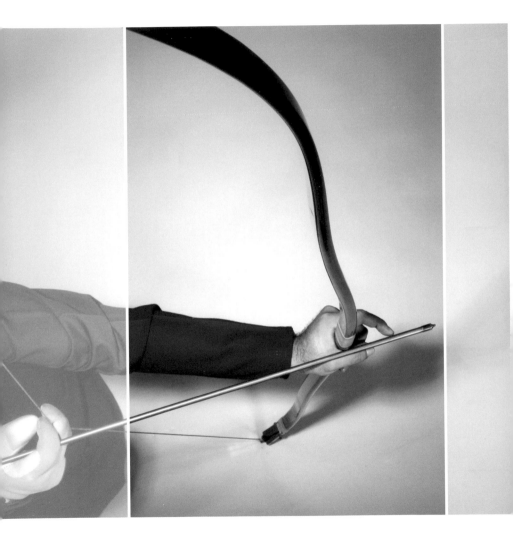

the japanese contribution to zen

Zen has given birth to many things. No other religious movement in the world has been so creative, so productive. It has created art that has a quality of its own, it has created poetry, it has created literature, it has created drama, it has created sculpture. Whatever it has created, it has left unmistakably the mark of meditativeness on it; it has turned things into meditation which nobody had ever imagined could even be associated with meditation.

ZEN WAS BORN in India in the absurd laughter of Mahakashyapa, a close disciple of Gautam Buddha. He had many disciples even closer than Mahakashyapa; Mahakashyapa is mentioned only once and that mention is of when he laughed.

This is the only mention of Mahakashyapa in the whole Buddhist canon. It is a vast literature, and for centuries, twenty-five centuries, people have been asking the question, "Why did Mahakashyapa laugh? And why was his laughter accepted? Not only accepted, but raised to the highest point of communication." Something transpired in that silent giving of the flower to Mahakashyapa. Zen became a new stream, flowing from Gautam Buddha to Mahakashyapa.

The next great name is Bodhidharma. His master told him to go to China, not to convert China to Buddhism... "But in China there is already a fragrance existing, created by Lao Tzu, Chuang Tzu, Lieh Tzu. Truth is nobody's

monopoly. It will be good if you take the treasure that Mahakashyapa has given from generation to generation to China. And let these two beautiful streams of mystics meet." Just as in crossbreeding the child is stronger, the same happens when two streams of thought, or of no-thought, meet, merge. Something new, far deeper than either, far greater than either arises.

It took Bodhidharma three years to reach China. He went to China and the crossbreeding happened. What was Zen in Buddhism was made even more simple, so that the Chinese could understand and use it. It flourished in China, and great masters arose out of the mystic experience. From China it was taken to Japan. Again a new crossbreeding.... And in Japan it is manifested in many dimensions.

There are two ways to disappear as a personality: one we can call "grounding" and one we can call "centering."

Mahakashyapa and Bodhidharma used centering: going within to the point where nothing remains but a pure presence, no person. The same approach became even more beautiful with the great heritage of Chuang Tzu, Lieh Tzu, and Lao Tzu. They were also people of centering. They were exploring their interiority to find themselves, and what they found was an absolute absence of anybody—even the finder disappeared. Out of that state came neither the found nor the finder, neither the seeker nor the sought, but an absolute silence, alive, full of its own music, full of its own dance. Seeing this, Mahakashyapa had laughed—"Buddha goes on saying to people 'Seek yourself, find yourself' and he is tricking them." It is a perfectly legitimate statement, to "seek yourself." But Mahakashyapa knew that when you find yourself, you are no longer there! It is a strange situation; except for laughter, nothing can express it.

There is an old definition of a philosopher: on a dark night, in a dark house where there is no light—and the philosopher, moreover, is blind—he is looking for a black cat which is not there. But the search continues. And if suddenly light comes in and his eyes are cured and he thinks of all the trouble that he was taking to find the cat which does not exist, what else is there to do except to laugh at himself?

Fools laugh at others. Wisdom laughs at itself.

In Japan the crossbreeding had a tremendous manifestation. Zen had come far from its beginnings in Mahakashyapa's laughter—a long journey. On the journey it gathered many new manifestations, many new revelations, many new methods. In Japan it finally turned out to be the peak. The peak is that anything can be used to find the truth. Even a warrior can use his sword, fighting with another warrior; there is no need for him to sit and meditate. The archer can find it in his archery; the painter can find it in his painting; the sculptor can find it in his sculpture.

What was in India only pure meditation grew in Japan into many branches. Indians cannot conceive how a warrior, a fighter with a sword, can be meditative, or how archery can be a meditative method, because Indians have

never tried it. Zen needed Mahakashyapa's laughter to travel from India to China and from China to Japan. On this long travel of a thousand years it gathered much insight.

One German professor, Herrigel, was reading about Zen and could not believe how the art of archery could be a form of meditation. There seems to be no relationship. Gautam Buddha sitting in the lotus posture meditating, that seemed to be perfect. But to conceive that an archer or a swordsman, whose effort is to kill the other, can be meditative...?

Herrigel went to Japan. For three years he was in Japan, and there he found the secret. He learned archery. He himself became an archer, a master archer, a hundred percent successful in hitting the target. But his Zen master said, "This is not the point. The point is not there in the target; the point is within you. Are you grounded?"

He said, "In the West we have practiced archery for hundreds of years and nobody has thought about grounding. What is grounding?"

The master said, "Grounding means you become almost part of the earth and allow the gravitation to flow in you, to flood you— particularly below the navel, two inches below to be exact. The gravitation comes from all around, and settles two inches below your navel."

But Herrigel asked, "What has this to do with archery? I have to concentrate on the target." The master said, "Forget about the target; first be grounded. And when you shoot your arrow, be relaxed, so that the gravitation shoots it, not you."

He said, "You are making strange statements. I will have to shoot. How can the gravitation shoot an arrow?"

Three years and Herrigel never missed a single target; he was a master archer. But his master would say, "No, you have still missed. I am not watching your target—who cares about your target? I am watching you; you are the target."

Why two inches below the navel? That is the center of life. It was from there that you were connected with your mother. It was from there that for nine months you were supplied with everything that you needed, and you didn't have to do anything at all—you were simply relaxed.

Grounding means bringing this life center within you into contact with the gravitational force, so that the gravitational force starts filling it. And a moment comes when you don't shoot at the target. Certainly you aim, but it is as if the arrow shoots itself. The gravitational force is enough to take it to the target.

Three years later Herrigel finally gave up. He said, "You are driving me crazy. Day and night I am thinking about how to do it." And the master said, "That's what I have been telling you! Don't *think* about how to do it, let it *happen*. Just have enough energy so it happens."

Finally Herrigel decided to go back. Three years are enough, and not even a single time had the master said, "Good." He always said, "You missed again." Every day Herrigel would come and every day he would be a failure. He told the master, "I am sorry, but I could not get the point. Tomorrow I am leaving, so I will come to say good-bye."

Next day he came. The master was teaching another disciple and Herrigel was sitting on the bench, simply watching, because it was not his business anymore; he was finished with it. If he could not get it in three years, he cannot get it in three lives. It is beyond any logic, what the master is saying.

So he was sitting relaxed, watching— watching the master because the master was showing the new disciple. And suddenly he saw the point. The master was so relaxed, it was not his hands that were shooting the arrow; it was so clear that some inner force was at work. Spontaneously he stood up, went to the master, took the bow and arrow, and shot the arrow.

For the first time the master said, "I can certify it—you have achieved. You were trying with your mind, tense. Today it was accidental—you were sitting relaxed, it was not your business, you were finished with it... And because you were finished with it, your eyes were clear, your heart was silent. You were watching in deep peace and silence, and you could see. For three years I was trying to show it to you, but could not because you were in a hurry to learn quickly and go back to Germany. Just now there was no hurry—you had already decided to go back to Germany.

"I can certify that you have achieved not only the art of archery, but simultaneously the art of grounding."

The moment you become grounded, as the trees are grounded—with deep roots in the earth—when your body is receiving forces from the earth and you are available, relaxed, allowing them to fill your life center, the mind stops functioning, time stops. So just by the side, meditation happens. People around the world have wondered, "What has meditation to do with archery?" But it happens. It can happen with anything. The question is that the mind should stop, time should stop; you should be relaxed and allow life to take possession of you.

I have always loved the story of a king who was passing through a village. He loved archery; he himself was a master archer. He could not believe that in that small village there lived someone who was certainly a greater archer than himself. He had not been one hundred percent; once in a while the target was missed. But there he saw circles on trees and exactly in the middle an arrow—on many trees.

He said, "This is... even the best archer cannot manage this. It seems so perfect. I want to meet the man." So he called the people and asked, "Who is the archer?" They

all laughed. They said, "Forget about him. He is the village idiot."

He said, "You don't understand. You bring him. His archery is perfect."

The villagers said, "You don't understand his archery. First he shoots the arrow and then he makes a circle around it. Naturally, he is perfect, always perfect. And we have told him, 'This is not the right way. First you should make the circle on the tree and then shoot. In that way one can miss. This is a simple way, you never miss.'"

Japan has been a warrior race, so naturally when Zen reached Japan it became associated with all kinds of swordsmanship, the art of archery, and other things. But they have retained the essential of Zen in it. Even Mahakashyapa would not be successful in archery, but that does not mean that he is not the originator.

I don't think Gautam Buddha would be able to pass Aikido examinations. He would be bound to fail. But that does not mean that Aikido is only a faraway echo of Gautam Buddha's experience of his own being. There is no contradiction.

Just remember one thing: whatever you are doing—chopping wood you can be a meditator, or carrying water from the well you can be a meditator—meditation is simply a silent thread inside you. You can do anything, and that silent thread should not be disturbed. Be careful that your awareness remains and then you can do anything.

In Zen, and only in Zen, something of great import has happened. That is, there isn't any distinction between ordinary life and religious life; rather, it has bridged them both. And Zen uses ordinary skills and methods for meditation. That is something of tremendous import. Because if you don't use ordinary life as a method to meditation, your meditation is bound to become something of an escape.

In India this has happened, and India has suffered badly. The misery that you see all around, the poverty, the horrible ugliness of it, is because India always believed religious life to be separate from ordinary life. So people who became interested in religion renounced the world. People who became interested in God closed their eyes, sat in the caves in the Himalayas, and tried to forget that the world existed. They tried to create the idea that the world is simply an illusion, illusory, a dream. Of course, life suffered much because of it.

All the greatest minds of India became escapists, and the country was left to the mediocre. No science could evolve; no technology could evolve.

But in Japan, Zen has done something very beautiful. That's why Japan is the only country where East and West are meeting: Eastern meditation and Western reason are in a deep synthesis in Japan. Zen has created the whole situation there. In India you could not conceive that swordsmanship could become a method for meditation, but in Japan they have done it. And in doing so, they have brought something new to religious consciousness.

Anything can be converted into a meditation because the whole thing is awareness. And of course, in swordsmanship more awareness is needed than anywhere else because life will be at stake every moment. When fighting with a sword you have to be constantly alert—a single moment's unconsciousness and you will be gone. In fact, a real swordsman does not function out of his mind; he cannot function out of his mind because mind takes time. It thinks, calculates. When you are fighting with a sword, where is time? There is no time. If you miss a single fragment of a second in thinking, the other will not miss the opportunity: the other's sword will penetrate into your heart or cut off your head.

So thinking is not possible. One has to function out of no-mind, one has to simply *function*, because the danger is so much that you cannot afford the luxury of thinking. Thinking needs an easy chair. You just relax in the easy chair and go off on mind trips.

But when you are fighting and life is at stake and the swords are shining in the sun and at any moment a slight unawareness and the other will not lose the opportunity, you will be gone forever, there is no space for thought to appear, one has to function out of no-thought. That's what meditation is all about.

If you can function out of no-thought, if you can function out of no-mind, if you can function as a total organic unity, not out of the head, if you can function out of your gut, it can happen to you. You are walking one night and suddenly a snake crosses the path. What do you do? Do you sit there and think about it? No, suddenly you jump out of the way. In fact, you don't decide to jump, you don't think

about it logically that "here is a snake; and wherever there is a snake there is danger; therefore, I should jump." That is not the way it happens—you simply jump! The action is total. The action is not corrupted by thinking. It comes out of the very core of your being, not out of your head. Of course, when you have jumped out of the danger you can sit under a tree and think about the whole thing—that's another matter! Then you can afford the luxury.

If the house catches fire, what do you do? Do you wonder whether to go out or not to go out—"to be or not to be"? Do you consult a scripture about whether it is right to do it? Do you sit silently and meditate upon it? You simply get out of the house. And you will not be worried about manners or etiquette—you will jump out of the window.

Just two nights ago a girl entered here at 3 A.M. and started screaming in the garden. Asheesh jumped out of his bed, ran—and only then realized that he was naked. Then he came back. That was an act out of no-mind, without any thought. He simply jumped out of the bed. Thought came later on. Thought followed, lagged behind. He was ahead of thought. Of course, it caught hold of him so he missed an opportunity. It would have become a *satori*— a glimpse of enlightenment—but he came back and put on his gown. Missed!

Swordsmanship became one of the basic methodologies in Zen, because it is so dangerous that it doesn't allow thinking. It can lead you toward a different type of functioning, a different type of reality, a separate reality. You know of only one way to function: to think first and then to act. In swordsmanship, a different type of existence becomes open to you: you act first and then you think; thinking is no longer primary.

This is the beauty—when thinking is not primary, you cannot err. You have heard the proverb, "To err is human." Yes, it is true, it is human to err because the human mind is prone to error. But when you function out of no-mind you are no longer human; you are part of the whole, and then there is no possibility of erring. The whole never errs, only the part; only the part goes astray.

When you start functioning out of nothingness, with no syllogism, with no thinking, with no conclusions—your conclusions are limited, they depend on your experience, and you can err—when you put aside all your conclusions, you are putting aside all your limitations also. Then you function out of your unlimited being, and it never errs.

It is said that sometimes in Japan two Zen people will fight who have both attained satori through swordsmanship. They cannot be defeated. Nobody can be victorious because they both never err. Before the other attacks, the first has already made preparations to receive it. Before the other's sword moves to cut off his head, he is already prepared to defend himself, and the same happens with the other. Two Zen people who have attained satori can go on fighting for years, but it is impossible for them to err. Nobody can be defeated and nobody can be victorious.

A TEMPLE FOR TEA— A ZEN CEREMONY

In Japan they have developed the tea ceremony. In every Zen monastery and in the house of every person who can afford it, there is a small temple for drinking tea. Now, tea is no longer an ordinary, profane thing; they have transformed it into a celebration. The temple for drinking tea is made in a certain way—in a beautiful garden, with a beautiful pond; swans on the pond, flowers all around…guests come and they have to leave their shoes outside. It is a temple.

As you enter the temple, you cannot speak; you have to leave your thinking and thoughts and speech outside with your shoes. You sit down in a meditative posture. The hostess, the woman who prepares tea for you, moves so gracefully, as if she is dancing, putting cups and saucers before you as if you are a god. With such respect, she bows down, and you receive it with the same respect.

The tea is prepared in a special samovar that makes beautiful sounds, a music of its own. It is part of the tea ceremony that everybody should listen first to the music of the tea. So everybody is silent, listening…birds chirping outside in the garden, and in the samovar the tea is creating its own song. A peacefulness surrounds all….

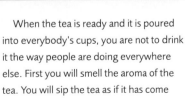

When the tea is ready and it is poured into everybody's cups, you are not to drink it the way people are doing everywhere else. First you will smell the aroma of the tea. You will sip the tea as if it has come from the beyond, you will take time—there is no hurry. An ordinary thing—plain tea—and they have made it a beautiful religious festival. Everybody comes out of it nourished, refreshed.

anecdotes of
the absurd

The truth cannot be contained by any word whatsoever.

The truth can only be experienced. The truth can be lived,

but there is no way to say it.

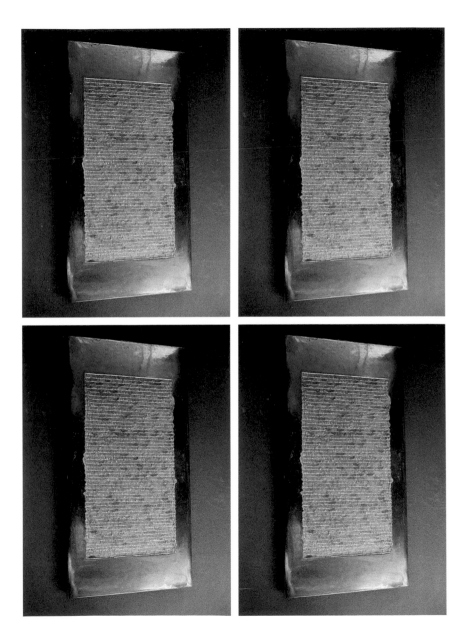

the illogical life

Zen is unique because no other religion exists on anecdotes. They are not holy scripture; they are simply incidents that have happened. It is up to you...if you understand them, they can open your eyes and your heart. These small anecdotes in their very smallness, just like dewdrops, contain the whole secret of the ocean. If you can understand the dewdrop, there is no need to understand the ocean—you have understood it.

Once a beginner asked a Zen master, "Master, what is the first principle?"

Without hesitation the master replied, "If I were to tell you, it would become the second principle."

THE FIRST PRINCIPLE cannot be said. The most important thing cannot be said, and that which can be said will not be the first principle. The moment truth is uttered it becomes a lie; the very utterance is a falsification. So all the scriptures of all the religions contain the second principle, not the first principle. They contain lies, not the truth, because the truth cannot be contained by any word whatsoever. The truth can only be experienced. The truth can be lived, but there is no way to say it.

The word is a far, faraway echo of the real experience. It is so far away from the real that it is worse than the unreal because it can give you a false confidence. It can give you a false promise. You can believe it, and that is the problem. If you start believing in some dogma, you will go on missing the truth. Truth has to be known by experience. No belief can help you on the way; all beliefs are barriers. All religions are against religion—it has to be so by the very nature of things. All churches are against God. Churches exist because they fulfill a certain need. The need is that people do not want to make any efforts; they want easy shortcuts. Belief is an easy shortcut.

The way to truth is hard; it is an uphill task. One has to go through total death—one has to destroy oneself utterly; only then is one newborn. The resurrection comes only after the crucifixion.

To avoid the crucifixion we have created beliefs. Beliefs are cheap. You can believe and yet remain the same. You can go on believing, and it doesn't require any basic change in your life pattern. It does not require any change in your consciousness, and unless your consciousness changes, the belief is just a toy. You can play with it, you can deceive yourself with it, but it is not going to nourish you.

Visualize a child playing in the garden of his house, playing with imaginary lions, and then suddenly he has to face a real lion who has escaped from the zoo. Now he does not know what to do. He is scared out of his wits. He is paralyzed; he cannot even run. He was perfectly at ease with the imaginary, but with the real he does not know what to do.

That is the situation of all those people who go on playing with beliefs, concepts, philosophies, theologies. They ask questions just to ask questions. The answer is the last thing they are interested in. They don't want the answer. They go on playing with questions, and each answer helps them to create more questions. Each answer is nothing but a jumping board for more questions. The

truth is not a question. It is a quest! It is not intellectual; it is existential. The inquiry is a gamble, a gamble with your life. It needs tremendous courage. Belief needs no courage. Belief is the way of the coward. If you are a Christian or a Hindu or a Mohammedan, you are a coward. You are avoiding the real lion; you are escaping from the real lion.

If you want to face the real, then there is no need to go to any church, there is no need to go to any priest, because the real surrounds you within and without. You can face it—it is already there.

I have heard:

A Zen master, Shou-shan, was asked by a disciple, "According to the scriptures, all

beings possess the Buddha-nature; why is it that
they do not know it?"
  Shou-shan replied, "They know!"

This is a rare answer, very rare, a great answer. Shou-shan said, "They know! But they are avoiding it." It is not a question of how to know the truth. The truth is here; you are part of it. The truth is now; there is no need to go anywhere. It has been there since the beginning, if there was any beginning, and it will be there until the end, if there is going to be any end. You have been avoiding it. You find ways to avoid it. When somebody asks, "What is the way to truth?" in fact he is asking, "What is the way to avoid the truth?" He is asking, "How can I escape?"

You may not have heard:

Says that old rascal Bodhidharma: "All know the way, few walk it, and the ones who don't walk cry regularly, 'Show me the way! Where is the way? Give me a map! Which way is it?' "

Those who don't walk go on regularly crying and shouting, "Where is the way?" Yet all know the way because life is the way, experience is the way. To be alive is the way; to be conscious is the way. You are alive; you are conscious. This is the first principle. But it cannot be said, and I am not saying it! And you are not hearing it.

The truth, by its very nature, is a dumb experience. All experiences are dumb because they happen only in deep silence. If you love a woman, the love happens in deep silence. If you create poetry, it descends on you in deep silence. If you paint a picture, you disappear. The painter is *not*, when the painting is born; there is not even a witness to it. It happens in utter silence and utter aloneness. If you are there, then the painting cannot be of any value. If the poet is there, then the poetry will be nothing but a technical thing. It will have all the rules fulfilled, it will follow the grammar, the rules of melody, but there will be no poetry. It will be a dead corpse. It will not be a real woman; it will be a nun.

I have heard:

At an isolated part of the beach of Cannes a beautiful French girl threw herself into the sea. A young man off at a distance noticed it and dashed into the water to save her, but it was too late. He dragged the seminude body ashore and left it on the sand while he went in search of an official. When he returned he was horrified to see a man making love to the corpse.

"Monsieur!" he exclaimed, "that woman is dead!"

"Sacré bleu!" muttered the man, jumping up. "I thought she was a nun."

To be a monk or to be a nun is to be dead. There are millions of ways to die and not live.

Truth surrounds you. It is in the air, it is in the fragrance of the flowers, it is in the flow of the river, it is in the green leaves, it is in the stars, it is in the dust, it is in you. Only truth is! But you go on avoiding it and you go on asking questions. How to attain to truth? Where is the map? Which way is it? And even if the map is given to you, the map does not help you in any way. In the first place, the map cannot be given, because the truth goes on changing. It is not a stagnant phenomenon; it is continuously changing. It is alive; it is breathing. It is never the same; it is never the same for two consecutive moments.

Says old Heraclitus, "You cannot step in the same river twice." In fact, you cannot even step once; the river is flowing, the river is flowing so fast. And not only is the river flowing, you are flowing. You cannot step in the same river twice: the river changes. You cannot step in the same river twice because *you* change.

Truth is dynamic. Truth is not something dead. That's why it cannot be contained in words. The moment you utter it, it has passed, it has gone beyond, it is no more the same. The moment you say it is so, it is no more so. Words lag behind.

To be with truth there is only one possibility: drop words. Language lags behind. Language is lame. Only silence can go with truth, hand in hand. Only silence can move with truth. Only silence can be so fast, because silence has no weight to carry.

Words are loaded; they carry weight. So when you are carrying words, great theologies in your head, great abstractions, then you cannot walk with truth. To walk with truth one has to be weightless. Silence is weightless; it has nothing to carry. Silence has wings. So only in silence is the truth known, and only in silence is the truth transferred, transmitted.

The tyro asked the Master:

"Master, what is the first principle?"
He must have been a tyro, a beginner; otherwise the question is foolish, the question is stupid. Either a stupid person or a philosopher can ask it. The question is meaningless because "first" means the most fundamental. The mind cannot contain it, because it contains the mind! The "first" means the basic; it was before the mind, so how can the mind comprehend it? Mind came out of it, mind is a by-product of it. The child cannot know the father; the father can know the child. The reality can know you, but you cannot know the reality. The part cannot know the whole; the whole can know the part. And the part cannot contain the whole. Now the mind is a very tiny part. It cannot contain the vastness of reality. Yes, the person who asked must have been a beginner.

"What is the first principle, Master?"
And the Master said:
"If I were to tell you, it would become the second principle."

Then it will be an echo, a reflection, a mirror image. Do you know who you are? You don't know, but you know your mirror image. You know your name, you know your address, you know the name of your family, the country, the religion, the political party you belong to. You know your face reflected in the mirror. You don't know your real face. You have not encountered your original face yet.

The Zen masters persist in telling their disciples, "Look into your original face—the face that you had before even your father was born, the face that you will have when you are dead, the face that is yours, originally yours."

All that we know about our face is not really about our face. It is the mask of the body, the mask of the mind. We don't know who lives in the body. We know truth as secondhand, borrowed.

Whenever something is borrowed it becomes ugly. Only the firsthand experience is beautiful, because it liberates. The secondhand thing is ugly because it becomes a bondage. If you become religious, you will be liberated. If you become a Christian or a Hindu or a Mohammedan, you will be in bondage. Mohammed was liberated because for him Islam was a firsthand experience. So was Jesus liberated because for him his experience was authentically *his* experience. Buddha was liberated; he came upon the experience. It was not handed to him by somebody else, it was not borrowed, it was not thought out, it was not a logical syllogism, it was not an inference. It was an experience!

Beware of inference. You have been taught inference to avoid experience. There are people who say, "God exists because if God is not there, who will create the world? God must exist because the world exists."

Just the other day I was reading a story about a rabbi:

A man came to the rabbi. The man was an atheist, and he said, "I don't believe in God, and you talk about God. What is the proof?" And the rabbi said, "You come back after seven days, and come wearing a new suit." The man said, "But what does that have to do with my question?" The rabbi said, "It has something to do with it. Just go to the tailor, prepare a new suit, and come after seven days."

The man came, reluctantly, because he could not see any relationship between his question and the answer that had been given. But he still came; he was wearing a new suit. The rabbi said, "Who has made this suit?" And the man said, "Have you gone mad? What type of a question are you asking? Of course, the tailor." The rabbi said, "The suit is here; it proves that the tailor exists. Without the tailor, the suit would not be here. And so is the case with the world. The world is here: there must be a tailor to it, a creator."

This is inference.

Change the scene. In a small Indian village a mystic is sitting with his disciples. Silently they are sitting; there is tremendous silence. It is a *satsang*—the disciples are drinking in the presence of the Master. And along comes an atheist, a scholar, a well-known logician, and he says, "I have come to ask one question. What is the proof of God?" The mystic opens his eyes, and he says, "If you want the proof of God, look into the eyes of the devotees. There is no other proof."

God exists in the eyes of the devotees. God exists in the vision of the lovers. It is an experience of the deepest core of your being, the heart. There is no other proof. God is not a concept. God is a reality, an experience, a deep subjective experience, the deepest there is. All else is peripheral.

" You enter into the temple, taking your shoes off,

and Zen believes,

'Where you leave your shoes, leave yourself too' "

God is the experience of your innermost center. When you are centered you know.

But you have been taught to believe in the God of the philosophers. That is a way to avoid the real God! The real God is very wild! The real God is very crazy! The real God is unknown and unknowable. And the real God cannot be controlled. The real God can possess you; you cannot possess the real. That is the fear: the mind is always afraid of anything that can possess it. The mind goes on playing games with words, ideas, philosophies. It can remain the master there. With the false, the mind is the master; with the real, the mind becomes a slave, and the mind does not want to become a slave. So the mind is completely contented with the secondhand.

Your God is secondhand. Your love, too, is secondhand. Your poetry is secondhand. Your dance is secondhand. Your singing is secondhand. And of course all these second-hand things make *you* secondhand; then you lose all originality.

Religion has nothing to do with logic. Religion has something to do with the first principle. Logic deals with the secondhand.

Logic deals with the junkyard, the used—used by many people. Logic deals with inference. And remember, it is good as far as the human world of intellectual garbage is concerned; the moment you go beyond that boundary, logic fails utterly, it falls flat on the ground.

I have heard a beautiful anecdote:

The safari had struck camp in dangerous territory and to protect themselves from wild animals they built a high fence around the camp. To be quite sure, they dug a deep ditch around the fence. One evening a member of the group, who was a professor of philosophy and a world-known logician, carelessly went out for an evening stroll without his gun and was attacked by a lion. He ran back to the camp with the lion after him and fell into the ditch. His friends inside heard a terrible yelling and screaming from outside, and when they ran out to look they saw the poor man—the poor philosopher—running round and round in the ditch closely followed by the lion. " Watch out, he is right behind you," they yelled down to him.

> *Zen is not interested in dogma. It is interested in helping you to contact your own being*

"That's all right," the philosopher yelled back. "I am one round ahead of him."

Logic is meaningless as far as life is concerned. Life is not logical at all; life is illogical. Logic is man-made, manufactured by the human mind. Life is absurd.

So if you go through inference you will reach the secondhand. If you go through experience you will reach the firsthand.

Religion is radical. Churches are not radical. The word *radical* means "belonging to the roots." Religious is radical, religion is rebellion. Churches are not rebellious; they are orthodox. Hence, I will repeat again, all churches are against religion. All so-called religious people are against religion. They deal in a false entity; they deal in counterfeit coins. That's why so many people look religious and there is not even a trace of religion on the earth. So many people talk about God, but it remains an empty talk.

Have you ever felt God? You have heard the word again and again and again. You are bored with the word. It has almost become a dirty word. From childhood people have been conditioning you for the word. Have you ever had any glimpse of God?

This is something very strange. How can we miss him? If he is the totality, if he is all over the place, how can we miss him? How did it ever become possible for us to miss him? We must have been doing great work to miss him. We must be doing much work to miss him. We must be avoiding him. We must be creating many barriers and hindrances and obstacles so that he cannot reach us.

And then these empty words: God, love, peace, prayer. All beautiful words have become empty. All ugly things are very real. War is real; love is unreal. Madness is real; meditation is unreal. Beauty is not there at all; ugliness, everywhere. You can come across the ugly any moment. But God is beauty, God is truth, God is love.

So what has happened? We have been trained for empty words, and we have become contented with these empty words.

Drop this contentment! If you want to know what is, become discontented with all that you have been taught, become discontented with all that you have been educated for! Become discontented with your education, with your society, with the power structures around you, the churches, the priests. Become discontented! Become discontented with your own mind. Only in that discontent comes a moment when you become capable of dropping all this mind and all this nonsense with it... and suddenly God is there, the first principle is there.

*A naive young man who had lived a
sheltered life finally decided he could not take
any more. He arranged an appointment with
his doctor and poured out the whole story.*

*"It is this girl I have been going with," he
said. "I suspected she was fast, but I never
dreamed she was a sex maniac. Every night
now for weeks and weeks on end, I keep trying
to break off the romance, but I haven't got the
will power. What can I do? My health just can't
stand the pace."*

*"I see," said the doctor grimly. "Tell me just
what happens; you can trust me."*

*"Well, every night I take her driving in
my car. We park in some secluded street. Then
she asks me to put my arms around her. And
then, every night, she reaches over and holds
my hand."*

"And then?"

*"What do you mean 'and then'?" gasped
the youth. "Is there more?"*

That's what has happened to religion.
The moment the word *religion* is uttered
you remember the long faces in the churches,
the sad-looking priests, the serious
theologians, trying to split hairs, chopping
abstract words, nobody knows why, for
what. Religion is broke. The religion of the
philosophers is bankrupt. The religion of
the intellectuals is relevant no more; it has
lost all relevance.

The old religion is dead! And it is good that it
is dead. The old God is dead! And it is good
that it is dead because now the door opens and
we can search for a new God: a God more real,

not conceptual, more existential, not
philosophical, a God who can be seen, loved,
lived, a God who can transform your life, a God
who is life and nothing else.

A different kind of religion is needed in the
world, a gut-level religion, a religion which has
blood and life, a religion whose heart still
beats. The old religion is dead, and people are
worshiping the corpse. The people carrying
the corpse, by and by, become just like the
corpse they are carrying.

The first principle is a gut-level religion,
a religion that you can experience in your
innermost core, in the interiority of your being.
You are the shrine for the first principle. No
Bible, no Koran, no Veda. You are the shrine for
the first principle. The only way to reach to the
real is to go within, to go in. Turn in.

That's what meditation is all about. That's
why Zen is not interested in dogma. It
is interested in helping you to contact your
own being.

When the fifth patriarch of Zen, Hung-jen,
was asked why he had chosen Hui-neng as his
successor out of the five hundred monks in his
monastery, he replied: "Four hundred and
ninety-nine of my disciples understood
Buddhism very well, and only Hui-neng had no
understanding of it whatsoever. He is not a man
to be measured by any ordinary standard.
Hence, the robe of authentic transmission
was given to him."

Because he has "no understanding of it
whatsoever." An intellectual understanding is
not an understanding. It is a deception, an
illusion, a dream, a substitute. Because you are

missing the real and because you are not courageous enough to accept the fact that you are missing the real, you substitute it. It is a plastic flower. You substitute the real with a false thing and then you feel good. You start thinking that you have it. And you don't have it! Your hands are empty.

Those four hundred ninety-nine disciples of Hung-jen were all scholars. For years they had studied all the scriptures. They had all the scriptures on their tongue. And he had chosen a man who has no understanding whatsoever. The man he had chosen, Hui-neng, was not known at all in the monastery. Nobody even was aware that he existed there.

When Hui-neng had come to the Master, the Master had asked him one thing: "Do you really want to know? Do you? Do you want to know about truth, or do you want to know truth itself?" And Hui-neng said, "What will I do by knowing *about* the truth? Give me the real thing." And the Master said, "Then go to the kitchen and clean the rice for the mess—and never come again to me. Whenever the right moment has come I will call you."

Twelve years passed, and Hui-neng was still working in the kitchen, at the back. People did not even know about him. Nobody knew his name. Who bothers to think about a man who works in the kitchen from the morning till late in the night? The monastery was not aware. There were great scholars, famous people, celebrities in the ashram: all over China their names were known. Who bothered about Hui-neng?

Twelve years passed, and then one day the Master declared, "My time has come and I will be leaving this world, so I have to choose a disciple as my successor. Anybody who thinks himself ready, capable of becoming my successor, should write four lines in front of my door to show his understanding." The greatest scholar went there in the night and wrote four lines, beautiful lines, the very essence of the *second* principle. You cannot reach higher through the mind than that. He wrote: "The mind is like a mirror. Dust gathers on it. Clean the dust, and you know what is." Perfectly true, absolutely okay. What more can there be?

The whole monastery was agog. People were discussing, debating whether the Master would choose this man as the successor or not. And everybody was trying to improve upon it, but nobody could find anything wrong in it. There was nothing wrong....

That is one of the most difficult things about the intellect. What is wrong in a plastic flower? Nothing is wrong. In a way—in many ways—it may be better than a real flower. A real flower is born in the morning and by evening it is gone. A plastic flower is more stable, more permanent—gives the idea of the eternal! The real flower is momentary. The real flower is born and dies, and the plastic flower knows no death. It is the closest that you come to the eternal. And what is wrong in it? It can have as much color as the real—more color because it is in your hands to make it so. You can make it perfumed, too. But something basic is missing; it is dead.

Nobody could find anything wrong. And people were trying to improve it, but they were all intellectuals. You cannot improve more than that; this is the last point the mind can reach. And it seems logical: "The mind is like a mirror. Dust gathers on the mirror, and then it cannot reflect"—that's what has happened to the mind.

Then a group of monks were discussing it, and they passed Hui-neng, who was doing his work in the kitchen. He heard it—they were talking about these beautiful lines, the essence of all the scriptures—and he laughed. For twelve years nobody had ever seen him laughing. He laughed. The monks looked at him and said, "What? Why are you laughing?" And he said, "It is all nonsense. It is not true." They could not believe their ears. This man, the rice cleaner, for twelve years just cleaning rice.... Nobody had ever seen him even meditating.

How can you see Deeksha meditating? Impossible.

One never knows.... This man, has he become enlightened or something? But they could not believe it, and they were scholars, so they laughed at the absurdity of it, and said, "All the great scholars are there, and you, a rice cleaner! For twelve years nobody has seen you reading scripture, studying, sitting by the side of the Master, inquiring about anything—can you improve upon it?"

Hui-neng said, "I can, but there is one problem. I cannot write. I knew twelve years ago, I used to write a little bit, but I have forgotten."

This happens; this unlearning happens. Unlearning is the process of becoming enlightened. Because you have learned wrong ways, and those wrong ways are the barriers, they have to be unlearned. You are born enlightened, and then you are forced into unenlightenment. You are conditioned for an insane society. Then you are forced to adjust to an insane society. If you remain miserable there is no wonder in it. You will remain miserable because this is not your real nature. This is not the flowering of your being.

So he said, "I cannot write. I have completely forgotten. If you can write, I can say something; you go and write it." Then he simply said, "The mind is not a mirror at all. Where can the dust gather? One who knows it knows it."

The mind is not a mirror. Where can the dust gather? One who comes to know this has known, has become enlightened, has looked into the deepest core of his being.

When these words were written on the door of the Master, the Master became very angry. Listen carefully—the Master became very angry. He said, "Bring this Hui-neng immediately, and I am going to beat him." The scholars were very happy; they said, "That's how it should be. Bring that fellow."

Hui-neng was brought, and the Master took him inside and told him, "So you have got it! Now you escape from this monastery. This is my robe; you are my successor. But if I tell it to people, they will kill you. It will be too much against their egos to accept a rice cleaner as the head of the monastery. You simply escape. That's why I was angry. Excuse me. I had to be. Escape from this monastery and go as far away as possible. You are my successor, but these people will kill you."

Scholars are very ambitious and political. Go to any university and you will see. Go to any academy and you will see. You will never see men anywhere else backbiting so much as in a university. Each professor against all, and each trying to pull everybody else down, and each thinks he is the only one capable of being the vice-chancellor or the chancellor. And all are fools.

Hui-neng escaped. Within two or three days people got the idea that something had happened. Hui-neng was missing, and the Master's robe was missing. They started searching for him. The greatest scholar, who had written the first lines, went in search. Hui-neng was caught in a forest, and when caught he said, "You can take this robe. I am not interested in this robe at all; this is absolutely unnecessary. I was happy cleaning rice. Now I am trying to escape and hide for no reason. You take this robe."

He dropped the robe on the ground, and the scholar tried to pick it up, but it was too heavy. He could not pick it up.

He fell on the ground perspiring, and said to Hui-neng, "Excuse me. I had come for the robe, but the robe is not ready to go with me. I am incapable. And I know that I am incapable because all that I know are words and words and words. Excuse me...and teach me something."

Hui-neng said, "Teaching is your problem; you have taught yourself too much. Now unteach, unlearn. Now drop all that you know. Knowledge is your barrier in knowing."

That's why the Master said "...and only Hui-neng had no understanding of it whatsoever." When you don't have any intellectual understanding, there arises a great understanding which is not of the mind, but which is of your total being. That understanding gives you the first principle, the first taste of tao.

I have heard:

A wealthy horse-owner died and left a large fortune to a university. A provision in the will, however, was that the school must confer the degree of Doctor of Divinity upon his favorite horse. Since the university was anxious to receive the money—it was a really big sum—the Dean set a date for the animal to receive a degree of DD.

This unusual occasion was attended by the press, and one of the reporters asked the Dean, "What is your reaction to this strange arrangement?"

"Well," replied the Dean, "in my experience I have awarded many degrees. However, I must admit that this is the first time I have awarded a degree to a whole horse."

All others were donkeys, not whole horses.

The mind cannot have any contact with reality. To live in the mind is to live like an idiot. To live with the mind, in the mind, as the mind, is to live a stupid life. The moment you become a little loosened from the mind: celebration. The moment you become a little loosened from the mind: joy. You become a little loosened from the mind: and God.

Suddenly the doors are open. They have never been closed; only your mind was blocking the way.

Thoughts don't allow you to see or, even if they allow, they distort. Or they interpret. They never allow the reality to come to you raw. They decorate it, they change it, they color it. They make it digestible to you. They make it according to you. And you are false, you are a mask, so when reality is cut according to you it becomes unreal.

That's why the Master said to the disciple, "If I tell you the first principle it will become the second principle. You are asking the question from the head." It was an intellectual question: "What is the first principle?" If the Master answered it, the head would take the answer, spin philosophy around it, and cause it to become the second principle.

The real, the true cannot be conveyed through words. It can be conveyed—yes, it can be conveyed—but the way to convey it is different. It is like measles: you catch them. Nobody can give them to you, but you can catch them. Truth cannot be taught but it can be caught.

Look at me. I have the measles. Now, if you don't resist, you will catch it, so lower your resistance. If you resist, you may not catch it. If you are really stubborn and hard and you close your being utterly, if you are not vulnerable at all, you will not catch it. But I cannot give it to you. You can catch it, or you can not catch it, but I cannot give it to you.

It cannot be given, but it can be taken, and that is the whole art of being with a master: to learn how to take. Because he will not give. He cannot give. He makes it available. A master is a catalytic agent; he is a presence. Something is possible around him. You have to be vulnerable,

The mind can give you the second principle. The first principle is possible only through no-mind. Meditation means a state of no-mind. Meditation does not mean "to think about." Meditation means not to think at all. It does not mean, of course, to fall asleep. It means to fall *awake*. It means thoughts should disappear and only pure consciousness should be there, a presence, a luminous presence: you see; there is clarity, transparency.

have an attitude of surrender, an attitude of receptivity: you have to be feminine.

Hui-k'o, another Zen master, made his way northward to H'sin-yeh, where he began teaching, and among those who came to hear him speak was Tao-ho, a noted teacher, a well-known author, and a famous scholar on Buddhist philosophy.

But Hui-k'o's teaching was not like that of any other Buddhist school's, and Tao-ho was very much disturbed....

The teaching was absurd, almost sacrilegious, because Hui-k'o used to say, "Kill your parents." A beautiful saying—but don't take it literally. The parents are within you. You can ask the T.A. (Transactional Analysis) people. The parents are within you. The mother, the father—their conditioning is within you. They control you from within. So when Hui-k'o said, "Kill your parents; only then come to me," he was uttering a great insight.

That's what Jesus said. Christians have not yet been able to explain it. He said, "Unless you hate your mother, unless you hate your father, you cannot come to me." Hate? And the utterance is coming from the man who says, "God is love"?

Hui-k'o also used to say, "If you meet the Buddha on the way, kill him immediately!" Because when you start meditating you will meet your parents; you will meet all the people who have been related to you. You will have to kill them; you will have to disassociate yourself from them; you will have to learn aloneness. And finally you will meet the Buddha, your Master, and you have to kill the Master, too.

These are dangerous things to say, and so is the way he used to say them. The scholar Tao-ho became very angry. He said, "This man will destroy all religion." That's what people say about me.

He determined to destroy this unholy doctrine and to that end dispatched several of his best students to dispute with Hui-k'o....

Hui-k'o is the successor of Bodhidharma, and of course he was a worthy successor of a great Master. He was a great disciple. Hui-k'o was attacked by this man Tao-ho in many ways. Tao-ho used to send his disciples to dispute with and to defeat Hui-k'o. Tao-ho awaited their return with high expectations of hearing that they had won a notable victory over the hated interloper, but they did not come back....

Not a single person ever came back. Whosoever went to Hui-k'o simply disappeared. These people are dangerous people. One should avoid them completely if one truly wants to avoid them. You may go as an antagonist, and you may fall in love with them. And these people are like dragons; once you are close to them they will suck you in.

Tao-ho sent out other emissaries, and still others, but none came back to report the expected victory. It was only after some time had passed that he met some of his messengers and said to them: "I had opened your eyes to the Tao; why were you such faithless emissaries?"

One of them spoke up for the rest: "The original eye is perfect in itself, but your teaching has rendered us half blind."

"The original eye is perfect in itself." Each child is born with that original eye—it is perfect—that innocent eye. It is perfect! It needs no improvement! And the effort of all the masters down through the ages has been one; whatsoever the society has done, they have to undo. Whatsoever the society has put into your mind, they have to take away. They have to dehypnotize you, they have to uncondition you. They have to make your childhood again available to you.

But remember, religion is not a teaching; it is not a learning. You can catch it. Yes, it is like measles. And you have to be in a mood to catch it. That mood is what is meant by being a disciple. A disciple shows a gesture, a great gesture, a *mahamudra*, that "I am ready, Master," that "I am open," that "I will not resist. If you are going to kill me, I am ready. Whatsoever you are going to do to me, I am available—my availability is total." That's all a disciple has to do. And the Master has to do nothing; he has just to be there.

The Master there—the one who has become enlightened, the one who has come to know his real nature—his presence, and the availability of the disciple, and something catches fire, something simply happens. That is the first principle. It cannot be asked, it cannot be answered. That which can be asked and that which can be answered will be the second principle; it will be a carbon copy, an echo.

Of course, the priests won't like such a rebellious meaning to be given to religion. They will not like people to become awake. Neither will the politicians like it.

The politician and the priest represent the ancient conspiracy against the innocence of humanity. They corrupt. Their business depends on this: that you remain unconscious, that you do not become aware. Because the moment you are aware, you are freedom—freedom from all politics and freedom from all religions. You are religious, but free from all religions. You cannot say that you are a Mohammedan, you cannot say that you are a Hindu.

To call Zen people Buddhist is wrong. It is as wrong as to call Sufis Mohammedans. It is as wrong as to call Hassidim Jews. The real people are simply real people. Zen, Sufi, or Hassid, there is neither Buddhist nor Mohammedan nor Jew.

But the priest will not like it. It will be destroying his business. It will be dismantling his shop, his whole market.

Two waiters were standing at a table over which a loaded customer had fallen asleep. Said one, "I have already awakened him twice. Now I am going to awaken him for the third time."

"Why don't you chuck him out?" asked the other waiter.

"The devil I will," said the first waiter. "I've got a good thing going for me. Every time I wake him up he pays his bill."

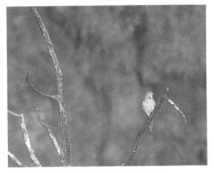

If humanity remains asleep, if humanity remains unconscious and hypnotized, then the politician can remain in power and the priest can go on exploiting you. If humanity becomes awake, then there will be no need for priests and politicians. There will be no need for any country or state, and there will be no need for any church, any Vatican, any pope. The need will disappear. There will be a totally different quality to human consciousness.

That quality needs to be born. We have come to the point in the evolution of human consciousness where this new consciousness is tremendously needed, desperately needed— this new consciousness which makes man free from politics and free from religion.

Let me remind you again and again, that will be the only religious world: free from religions, but not free from religion; free from churches and dogma, but not free from the first principle; free from all the second principles.

> *When you are happy,*
>
> *you start disappearing*

A girl told her friend she had just become engaged to a traveling salesman.

"Is he good looking?" asked the friend.

"Look, he would never stand out in a crowd."

"Does he have money?" continued the friend.

"If he does, he won't spend it."

"What about his bad habits. Does he have any?"

"Well, he drinks an awful lot," said the future bride.

"I don't understand you," said the friend. "If you can't say anything nice about him, then why are you marrying him? "

"He is on the road all the time," she replied, "and I will never see him."

That's the only good thing about it—and that is the good thing about the god of the priests: you will never see him. That's why you go on following the priest. To avoid God, you follow the priest. To avoid God, you read the Bible. To avoid God, you chant Vedas. To avoid God, you become scholars, thinkers. To avoid God, you are doing everything that is possible.

But why do you want to avoid God? Why in the first place do you want to avoid God? There are reasons. The very idea of God creates tremendous fear because God will mean death to your ego. You will not exist if God is there.

The great Indian mystic Kabir has said, "Look at the irony of it. When I was, God was not; now God is, I am not. Anyway, the meeting has not happened." Because for the meeting, two are needed. "When I was, God was not; now God is, I am not."

The fear is that you will have to lose yourself. You are afraid of death; that's why you are afraid of God. And that's why you are afraid of love, and that's why you are afraid of all that is great.

You are too attached to this false ego which never gives anything but misery and pain, but at least gives you a feeling that you are. Just watch. Meditate over it.

If you want to be, then you will always fall into the trap of the priest. In fact, you are not. The whole idea is a false notion. How can you be? The waves exist, but not separate from the ocean. So we exist: not separate from the ocean of consciousness. That's what God is. The leaves exist, but not separate from the tree. Everything exists, but nothing exists separately.

No man is an island and no part can exist independently. We exist in deep interdependence. We are members of one another, of each other. We penetrate each other. This whole existence is a great penetration. Trees penetrate you; you penetrate the trees. Stars penetrate you;

you penetrate the stars. You penetrate the earth; the earth penetrates you. Everything is penetrated.

God is this totality. You cannot exist separately. If you want to exist separately, then you are a politician. All politics are nothing but the shadow of the ego. Then you will live in misery and in madness.

But if you look, if you watch deeply, you will be surprised. You are not! Not that you have to dissolve! Simply you are not. It is just a false notion that you have been carrying, the notion that you are. Any moment of silence and you will suddenly see there is emptiness within you, nothingness within you. Buddha has called this nothingness *anatta*, nonbeing, *shunya*, nothingness. If you look within, you will not find yourself. That's why people don't look within; they are afraid.

Once it happened that I was traveling with Mulla Nasruddin on a train. Came the ticket collector and Nasruddin became very hectic. He looked in his suitcase, he turned over all the things, he looked in the bed, turned over everything, he looked in his many pockets, and he started perspiring and he could not find the ticket. I saw that he had not looked in one pocket, so I told him, "Nasruddin, you have not looked in that pocket." He said, "Don't mention that." I said, "But why? The ticket may be there." He said, "Don't mention it at all. If I look in it and the ticket is not found, I will fall dead. I will drop dead! I cannot look in that pocket! If the ticket is not there, then I am finished. There is a hope that it may be there."

That's why people don't look inside: a hope one may be there. The day you look in, you are not. The day you look in, suddenly there is vast emptiness...and it is tremendously blissful, beautiful, peaceful. You are not there; then there is no noise.

That's what Hui-neng means when he says, "There is no mirror of the mind. Where can the dust gather? To know this is to know all."

Look within. People think, "We are bad," but you are not, so how can badness gather? People think, "We are good," but how is it possible? You are not there; how can you be good? People think, "We are moral and immoral and this and that," but everything hangs on the idea of "I." To be good the "I" is needed first; to be virtuous the "I" is needed first. To be a sinner or to be a saint the "I" is needed first. Without the "I" you will not have anything to hang anything upon. Where will you hang your goodness, your sin, or your saintliness?

That's why Zen insists there is nobody who is a sinner and there is nobody who is a saint, nothing is good and nothing is bad. All distinctions are ego-created. Distinctions are created so that the ego can exist through the distinctions. When you look within there is neither saint nor sinner, neither good nor bad, neither life nor death. All distinctions disappear.

In that nothingness one becomes one with God. One *is* one with God—one has been from the very beginning. So the fear is that if you want to know God, you will have to disappear; so you don't look into your own being. The fear is that if you look within yourself you may become happy.

People say that they want to become happy, but I rarely come across a person who really wants to be happy. People cling to their misery. Again the same game. With the misery you have something to do. With the misery, some occupation. With the misery you can avoid yourself, you are engaged. With joy there is nothing with which to be engaged, there is nowhere to go. In joy you again disperse and disappear. In misery you are there—you are very much there. Misery gives you a solid experience that you are. When you are happy, you start disappearing. When you are really happy, you are not, again you are not. In a state of bliss, again you disappear.

You talk about heaven, but you go on creating hell because only in hell can you exist. You cannot exist in heaven. George Bernard Shaw is reported to have said, "If I am not going to be the first in heaven, then I would not like to go to heaven. I would like to be in hell, but I would like to be first; I don't want to be second." Hell is okay, but the ego says, "Be first, be a leader." Hell is okay if the ego remains; heaven is not okay if the ego has to be dropped.

You would like to be in heaven with your ego. You are asking the impossible. That cannot happen.

The religion that exists on the earth is false, it is a make-believe, it is just for the name's sake, but it fulfills your demand. It fulfills a certain demand, that you want to pretend that you are religious. You don't want to become religious but you want to pretend. And you want to pretend in such a way that not even you yourself can catch yourself pretending.

You want to pretend in such a way that you don't ever come across your pretensions, so a great structure is created. And that great structure is the church. Avoid that structure if you really want to become religious. And unless you are religious you are not!

Now let me tell you this paradox: You are only when you are not, because you are only when the ego has disappeared and you are God. That is the first principle. I am not telling it to you, and you are not hearing it from me.

It happened:

The car suddenly broke down in the middle of nowhere. He crawled underneath to see what the trouble was. She crawled underneath to hold the flashlight for him.

It was quite cozy under there and, after a while, they forgot about car repairs. Suddenly a voice said, "And just what do you two think you are doing?"

Looking up, they saw the local village constable.

"Why, we are—er—repairing the back axle," the young man stammered.

"Well, while you are down there, you had better look at the brakes as well," replied the law. "Your car has been at the bottom of the hill for the past half hour."

That's what has happened to churches. Jesus is not there; Buddha is not there. People are doing something else in the name of Jesus,

in the name of Buddha, and they are thinking Buddha is there. Church is the last place where you can meet Jesus, and the Buddhist temple is the last place where you can meet a buddha. But you go to the church, you go to the temple...and you think you are going to Buddha and to Jesus.

You are great pretenders. You want to pretend. You want to be respectable. You want to show to everybody that "We are religious people." So we have created a Sunday religion; every Sunday you go. Six days for the world; one day—not the whole day, just one or two hours—for God. Just in case something goes wrong or maybe really God is or maybe one survives death. These are all perhapses. And a perhaps never changes anybody's life; only a certainty changes somebody's life.

Hence, my insistence, if you cannot find a living master, go on searching and searching. There are always living masters somewhere or other; the earth is never empty of them. But never go to the places where conventionally you expect them. There they are not. Jesus was not in the synagogue. Buddha was not in any Hindu temple; he was born a Hindu, but he was not in any Hindu temple. Jesus was a Jew, but he was not in the synagogue. And so has been the case always. Don't go on worshiping ideas. Find a living reality.

The moment you find a living reality, become vulnerable, become open. And you will have the first principle, which cannot be said, but you can get it.

zen
dialogues

All these Zen anecdotes and dialogues say the same thing again and again. But they say it very beautifully. From different standpoints, from different attitudes, they point to the same moon... hoping that perhaps, if last night you did not see it, today it may be possible from some other aspect.

tales of enlightenment

These stories belong to a world, to a time, when people were simple. They were not cunning or complex; they were innocent. Hence there was a possibility of immediate awakening. Zen has become more and more difficult for the simple reason that man has become more and more complex. Today it is almost impossible to conceive how sudden enlightenment can be possible, how in a single flash of lightning one can be transformed totally. The knowledgeable person can only understand the way of gradualness; his whole education is a process of graduation.

ZEN IS SPECIAL in many ways compared to other traditions of the mystics. But what stands out, unique, are the strange, small dialogues in Zen: just reading them you cannot see how those small dialogues can bring enlightenment to someone.

Secondly, Zen itself gives no explanations. That is one of the reasons a living tradition of enlightenment has not overtaken the world. I would like you to understand these small dialogues which apparently mean nothing, but in a certain circumstance produced by other Zen methods can bring awakening. The dialogues are remembered down the centuries, and the people on the path of Zen enjoy them immensely.

However, for outsiders they remain a mystery because the context is never told; in what reference the awakening happened is never discussed.

Behind these small dialogues there is a long discipline of meditation and understanding—maybe years and years of work. But only the dialogue is known to the outside world. You don't know those who are discussing with each other; they are not ordinary people. The awakening is possible only if they have a background that can make the small piece of dialogue—which in itself is nothing—of tremendous importance. But when you read them, you cannot believe how these dialogues can make somebody enlightened—because you are reading them and you are not becoming enlightened!

Something is missing in your perspective. My effort will be to give you the entire context and to explain not only the words of the dialogue but also the individuals who are engaged in these small dialogues. Only then will you see that they are not small things, they are the very essence. The people involved have reached to the

ultimate point; these dialogues are just a little push. They were almost ready... it can be said that even without these dialogues they were going to become enlightened, maybe a week later. These dialogues have cut no more than a week from the time of their being enlightened.

Now that Zen has become fashionable all around the world there is so much written about it. But nobody I have come across up to now...and I have seen almost everything that has been written about Zen by people who don't have any enlightenment, but who are impressed by the beauty of the people who have been following Zen. They have picked up things that make no sense, are almost nonsense, and they don't have the capacity to give you the background.

Remember, everything depends on the background: long years of preparation, long years of waiting and longing, long years of

silent patience and meditating. The dialogue comes at the apex, at the very end. If you can understand the whole process, then it will be clearer to you how the dialogue can bring enlightenment to someone.

Unless people know the whole process, Zen will remain just entertainment to the world. What is enlightenment to Zen people falls down to a state of entertainment. These dialogues are not the whole process. It is just like an iceberg: a small piece is showing above the sea—one-tenth of the iceberg—and nine-tenths is underneath. Unless you understand that nine-tenths, the one-tenth will not give you any insight.

The first dialogue:

In the old days the venerable Yen Yang asked Chao Chou, "What is it like when not bringing a single thing?"

Chou said, "Put it down."

Yen Yang said, "Since not a single thing is brought, put what down?"

Chou said, "If you can't put it down, pick it up."

At these words, Yen Yang was greatly enlightened.

Now, if you hear only this small anecdote, you cannot imagine how it can possibly bring great enlightenment.

First, in the context of the Zen approach—in the eyes of Gautam Buddha and Bodhidharma—the world is nothing but emptiness. And when they use the word *emptiness*, they have their own meaning; it is not the ordinary meaning that you can find in a dictionary. If everything is removed from your room—all the furniture, the photographs hanging on the wall, the chandelier and everything—and nothing is left behind, anybody will say, "This room is empty." This is the ordinary meaning of the word. But from the perspective of Gautam Buddha, this room is empty of things but it is full of space. In fact, when things were there, they were hindering the space. The very word *room* means "space." So it is overflowing now with space, with nothing to hinder, nothing to prevent and obstruct the space.

Space is not a negative thing like the word *emptiness* connotes. Everything in the world has come out of space and everything disappears into space. Space seems to be the reservoir of all that is....

Scientists have discovered black holes in space. It is the most amazing story that science has to tell. The scientists themselves feel mystified, but what can they do? They have come across a few places in space where the moment any star, even the biggest, comes into that area, you can no longer see it: it has become pure nothingness. The pull of these few places is so tremendous that anything that comes close to them is immediately pulled into the black hole and disappears from the world. Every day, many stars disappear into black holes; that is the basic idea.

But then, certainly, scientists started thinking: if there are black holes, there must be white holes, too. If everything goes on disappearing into the black holes, one day everything will have disappeared. But every day new stars are being born—from where do they come? It is still an assumption, a hypothesis, that from wherever they come, that place should be called a white hole.

My own understanding is that the black hole and the white hole are just two sides of the same phenomenon; they are not separate. It is just like a door: you can go in, you can go out. On one side of the door is written "Push" and on the other side is written "Pull."

The black hole de-creates; it is a death. Not only do you get tired and old, now they say even metal gets tired; even for machinery, working twenty-four hours a day is too much. You are creating too much tension in the metal. It needs a little rest to recover itself; otherwise, soon it will not be functional anymore. Even machines become old, just as people do.

Stars become old, just like everything else. When a star or a planet has become too old and cannot hold itself together anymore, it disappears into a black hole. Its death has come. It is a de-creation. The function of the black hole is to disperse all constituents of the planet or star—to return them to their original form.

The original form is electricity, energy, so matter melts into energy. Energy cannot be seen, you cannot see it. Have you ever seen electricity? You have seen a byproduct of electricity, like your light bulb, but you have not seen electricity itself. When it is passing through a wire, do you see anything? And if the bulb is removed, the electricity is still there, but do you see it?

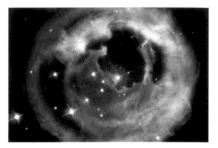

No energy can be seen. No energy is visible, so when the mass of a vast star or planet falls back into the original source, it becomes pure energy. That is why you cannot see it: it has disappeared. Perhaps it was time for a long rest. And once it is rested, then the basic constituents can again come together, can again form a new body and get out into the universe from the other side of the black hole—that is, the white hole.

This is significant. It means the universe is continuously renewing itself in the same way as every individual is born, grows old, dies, and then somewhere else is born in a new form, fresh, young. This is the process of rejuvenation.

Existence itself is full of space. Space looks empty to us, but it is not empty, it is a potential for things to happen. Everything has come out of it—how can you call it empty? Can you call a mother's womb empty? It

has the potential of giving birth to life. It appears empty because its potentiality has not been transformed into actuality.

Gautam Buddha was the first man to use the word *emptiness* in the sense of spaciousness, infinite space. Everything is just a form, and the thing that is creating the form is invisible. Only the form is visible; the energy that makes it is invisible.

The Zen disciple meditates continuously on the emptiness of existence, on the spaciousness of existence. All forms are empty; no form has a self. Only existence has a self. All others are only dreams lasting for a few years—and in the eternity of time, a few years are not much to brag about; they don't matter at all. The meditator continually goes on and on realizing the nature and the flavor of nothingness.

One day he understands that everything phenomenal that appears will disappear—today it exists, tomorrow it may be gone—it is nothing eternal. And unless something is eternal, it is not real.

Getting deep into this meditation will change your whole life. Anger comes and you know that it is just an energy form; you don't pay attention to the person against whom you are angry. The meditator pays his whole attention to anger itself. The form disappears, and the energy contained in the form is absorbed by the meditator.

As things go on disappearing—sadness, tensions, unhappiness, misery—you go on becoming more and more powerful, because everything is falling back into the form of energy. In this state, try to understand the anecdote.

The second dialogue:

Master Shui Lao asked Ma Tsu, "What is the true meaning of the coming from the West?"

Ma Tsu then knocked him down with a kick to the chest: Shui Lao was greatly enlightened. He got up, clapping his hands and laughing loudly, and said, "How extraordinary! How wonderful! Instantly, on the tip of a hair, I've understood the root source of myriad states of concentration, and countless subtle meanings." Then he bowed and withdrew.

Afterward, he would tell the assembly, "From the time I took Ma Tsu's kick up until now, I haven't stopped laughing."

A sudden rain shower after a long dry spell can be an immense joy...not only to the earth, which is thirsty, waiting for it—but also to the trees and to all the people. Such small experiences can release in you the ultimate experience...just the beauty of them, the splendor, unexpected, unpredictable. Suddenly you are surrounded with tremendous peace, silence—not empty, but full of songs and dances, and the whole existence rejoicing.

As one goes deeper on the path, as one releases oneself from the prison of one's own mind, ordinary experiences start taking on extraordinary colors. An ordinary flower looked at silently becomes a wondrous experience. What a marvel that a small flower can exist with such beautiful colors, with a little fragrance of its own, an individuality of its own. The greatest philosopher cannot fathom the meaning of the smallest flower.

But the mystic is not a philosopher; he does not bother to fathom meanings, to measure meanings, to think about things. He simply rejoices in them. When it rains, he dances, he joins hands with the rain. When trees are rejoicing, becoming fresh, one starts feeling the same freshness. Only one thing is needed, and that is the offering of this small story...release.

This small dialogue is intended to convey a simple thing to you: you are the prison, you are the prisoner, and you are the one who has imprisoned you. You are playing a game with yourself. One part of you functions as the jailer, another part functions as the jail, and your innermost core is crushed between these two parts. You become a prisoner; it is not that somebody else is making you a prisoner.

It would have been a great calamity if human consciousness were imprisoned by somebody else. Then freedom would not be in your own hands; then freedom would be in somebody else's hands. It is marvelous that you are yourself imprisoning your being; hence, the release can happen instantly. It is only a question of a little understanding, a little intelligence.

Many intellectuals in the world who have become aware of Zen in the past century were, in the beginning, simply laughing at the craziness of these people, because it did not make sense to their reasoning minds. Somebody hits you and you become enlightened...the mind cannot believe it. There seems to be no reason why a certain hit would destroy all your ignorance.

Even today, Zen is being studied in the West on a vast scale; it has become one of the universal phenomena. But the very idea of studying it goes against it: you cannot study Zen. You can have it, but you cannot get it from someone else. And the simple reason is that you have it already. It is just a question of forgetfulness. It will be helpful for you to be reminded. Perhaps in everybody's life there are moments when you know that a certain name, a certain person, a certain face is known to you. The expression exists in all languages that it is "just on the tip of my tongue."

Then who is preventing you? Why don't you tell it? You know perfectly well it is there, but it needs some release, and perhaps a hit may do it. You have only forgotten—perhaps a good hit will help you to forget to remember it, because the effort to remember a thing makes your mind tense, and the more you try to remember, the more tense you become.

Tension means narrowing of the mind. It becomes so narrow that nothing can pass through it. A good hit and the mind opens... because you have forgotten that you were trying to remember something, and suddenly that which was on your tongue is no more a secret; now you know it fully well. Something like this has been happening in transmissions of a higher and deeper level.

But Zen is not a study. There is no way to make it a subject of studies in the universities; that would be stupid. There is no way to find someone who has it who can give it to you. It is not that the people who have it are miserly or not generous—just the contrary. They are the

most generous people; if they could give it to you they would not bother whether you want it or not, they would give it to you.

But the very nature of the experience is such that it does not come from outside; it happens within you. The people who have experienced it are in constant search of creating a situation around you so that what is asleep becomes awake. Once you understand it, Zen will not look crazy; it will not look irrational. It will look super-rational—beyond the capacities of the mind.

Hindus, Mohammedans, Christians, and Jews have created a difficult situation for millions of people. They have been giving people the idea that it will be delivered to you by a savior, it will be given to you by a messenger; all you have to do is to believe and wait. Jesus will redeem you, or Mohammed, or Krishna.

What I want to point out very clearly is that the idea that somebody else, it does not matter who—Jesus, Moses, Krishna, or Mohammed—the idea that somebody else will do it on your behalf is absolutely wrong. But this idea has prevailed and it is easy to accept it, it is simple to be imprisoned by it because somebody else is taking the responsibility.

In this world, people are easily ready to give responsibility to somebody else. They think that by giving away responsibility they are free of the burden. They are absolutely wrong. Responsibility *is* freedom, and the moment you give responsibility to somebody else you have also given your freedom.

Now two thousand years have passed and Christians are waiting for the savior to come. I tell you he is never going to come, for the simple reason that what he has promised he cannot deliver. Krishna has promised that he will be coming, but it is strange that nobody wonders why these people did not redeem humanity while they were here. What is the point of postponing it for the future, for the next time they come?

People were as much in misery then as they are now, people were as ignorant as they are now—so what was the reason to postpone? Jesus could have redeemed the whole world; Krishna could have enlightened everybody. But it was a subtle game: they

took the responsibility and helped you to remain a prisoner till they come back. Just go on praying...one day he is going to come.

This has taken away not only your responsibility but also your freedom. It has taken away your individuality and your uniqueness.

I love Gautam Buddha for the simple reason that he is the first man in the long history of humanity who refused to take the responsibility of redeeming anybody. He seems to be the most courageous man—because it is so easy to gather followers if you take responsibility. But rather than taking responsibility, he was saying that there is no way for anybody else to redeem you.

Let it sink deep in your heart. Only you are capable of awakening, because only you are capable of falling asleep. Nobody else is responsible for your sleep—how can somebody else be responsible for your awakening? All those who have promised to redeem you have reduced you to something less than human beings. Jesus was calling himself the shepherd and people the sheep and I sometimes wonder why not even a single person stood up and said, "This is very insulting." Not that people must not have felt it, but it was very cheap, and "this fellow is taking all the responsibility, that is good—so we need not bother about it. We can go round and round in our trivia and he will take care of our spirituality." It was a good chance to get rid of the whole affair. It seems hurtful to say it, but I cannot say anything that is not true. All these people behaved more like businessmen; they were concerned with having more and more customers.

Gautam Buddha seems to be the only man who was not interested in having followers, who was not interested in being a shepherd, who was not interested in reducing people to sheep. On the contrary, his whole life he insisted on only one thing: You are just like me; the difference is very small. One day I was asleep, today I am awake. Today you are asleep, tomorrow you may be awake—and if you are intelligent you can be awake this very moment.

Gautam Buddha, rather than talking about hypothetical nonsense, took on the existential problem directly: the problem is your release. And the problem is simple because the release is within your own hands: you have just forgotten who you are. By telling you who you are, you will not understand, and the danger is that by telling you who you are, you may become a parrot. In India you will find a whole country full of parrots. Everybody is talking about the soul, enlightenment, awakening, nirvana. They have all been repeating beautiful sentences from scriptures. Buddha does not want to make you a parrot; hence, he says there is no way to give you the truth, for the simple reason that you already have it.

So all that can be done is somehow to create situations to wake you up and, if it is needed, to give you a good slap at the right moment. Anybody's slap won't do, only a master's—and only a disciple who has been working on the way for years, or maybe for lives, comes to a point just on the boundary line, where a little push…and he has reached to the other shore. So there are disciplines in Buddhism, but those disciplines are not going to give you the truth. They are only going to bring you to the point where some insightful and compassionate master will be needed to create a device which releases you.

Have you seen young birds? They see their parents flying all around, and they also flutter their wings. But they are afraid—naturally, because they have never flown—and they cannot believe that going out of their cozy nest is safe.

The vast sky and no experience of flying frighten them—although they are capable of flying, they have the wings, and they will rejoice to fly in the sky under the warm sun.

Finally the parents of those small birds have to push them. That is a device—that is a Zen device. But the parents have to wait until their wings are strong enough; they do many things which to me seem to be exactly what the Zen master does for the disciple. The mother will fly in front of them, showing that if she can fly, why can't they? The young birds flutter their wings to gain confidence, to become acquainted with the fact that they also have wings—it's true!

But to take the jump…. They come to the very edge of their nest. They weigh all the pros and cons. There is a great longing to take the jump, but there is also a fear because they are going into the unknown. Who knows—they may fall flat on the earth and be finished. The mother goes to the other tree, and from there she starts calling them: Come on! It is irresistible. They try, but some invisible boundary prevents them.

When the parents see that they are perfectly capable and it is only fear that is preventing them, one day, without informing them, suddenly—a Zen push!

Of course, in the beginning they flutter haphazardly, but they know now that although they are not flying as they should, they can keep themselves up in the air. Then the mother starts calling to them from other trees. First they go to close trees, then they start going to farther trees, and one day they are gone forever into the infinite; they never come back. Then the whole sky has become theirs.

I have always thought that the Zen devices of transmitting must have come from such sources. Zen monasteries are in the forests, and some genius master may have seen the situation of a bird being pushed. There is no logical sense to it, you cannot convince the bird intellectually, and a push is not rational. Only in principle is it sudden enlightenment. In practice, in reality, the small bird has to grow strong wings, wait for the right moment, and has to be under the protection of a right master. Any hurry can be fatal.

If somebody is awakened before his ripening time, before his maturity, that enlightenment can be dangerous. He may not be able to survive it, it may be too much. He was not yet able to contain it, to absorb it, to relish it.

Intellectuals all over the world have asked, "If it is sudden, then why is it not happening to us? Then why does somebody have to meditate for years if it is sudden?" They have not understood that *in principle* it is

sudden. When it happens, it will happen suddenly—but before that happening, a certain maturity is needed. That means enlightenment in itself is sudden, but the preparation for it is gradual.

Gradualness and suddenness are not necessarily opposite; that gradualness can be a preparation for suddenness. Both can be part of a synthetic process. It takes time, different times for different people. According to their love, according to their trust, according to their longing, according to their passion, according to their readiness to risk all, the time element will differ.

When one comes to a master, one has so much garbage that the master has to remove it gradually, because to him it is garbage, but to the disciple it is knowledge. To the master it is chains; to the disciple, these are his ornaments. So it takes time...the master throwing the garbage out and the disciple collecting it back, and hiding it in deeper places where the master cannot reach, until there is a recognition that the master and the disciple stand in the same space. Then anything will do, even a little push.... So you have to just remain alert and aware—not aware of anything special, not of any object, but just alert, as if something great is going to happen and you don't know what. As if a great guest is going to come and you are standing at your door waiting. You don't know who is coming...you don't know whether he is coming or not. You don't have any confirmation—but greatly alert, you are standing at the door. A pure awareness...

Master Shui Lao asked Ma Tsu, "What is the true meaning of the coming from the West?" This is a special way of asking the question, "What is the true meaning of Bodhidharma coming from the West?" because to China, India is the West. "What was the special reason for Bodhidharma coming to China?" In other words, the question is, "What has he come to transmit?" It took him three years to reach that far, and it took him nine years to transmit it. What was it?

Ma Tsu then knocked him down with a kick to the chest: Shui Lao was greatly enlightened. He got up, clapping his hands and laughing loudly, and said, "How extraordinary! How wonderful! Instantly, on the tip of a hair, I have understood the root source of myriad states of concentration, and countless subtle meanings." Then he bowed and withdrew.

Afterward he would tell the assembly, "From the time I took Ma Tsu's kick, up until now, I have not stopped laughing."

Remember that Master Shui Lao is not an ordinary disciple; he is already recognized as a great master, although he is only a great teacher. But the difference is subtle and can be known only by those who are beyond the master and the teacher. He was known as a master himself...and he was not just a teacher; he had come gradually closer and closer to being a master but he needed a last push. He was fluttering his wings... he was waiting, but on the verge of flying into the sky.

> *The master is there not only to teach you certain doctrines; he is there to release you from the prison that you yourself have made*

Master Shui Lao asked Ma Tsu... Ma Tsu is one of the strangest masters in the assembly of strange masters of Zen. Shui Lao is asking a simple question: "Why did Bodhidharma come to China? What special transmission was there that he had to deliver?"

Ma Tsu then knocked him down with a kick to the chest: Shui Lao was greatly enlightened.

Now incidents like this make intellectuals confused. What has happened? Ma Tsu has shown him that Bodhidharma has come to kill your ego, to release you from the fear of death. He kicked him in the chest, knocked him down. It was so strange and so sudden, it was not expected. He had asked a simple, routine question; any intellectual could have explained why Bodhidharma had come to China—to spread Buddhism, to spread the message of the great master.

Nobody could have thought that Ma Tsu would do this to the poor questioner, but it only seems sudden and unpredictable to us; Ma Tsu could have seen the ripeness of the

man, his maturity...that he needed just a small push, that this moment should not be missed. Kicking him on the chest and knocking him down may have completely stopped the functioning of his mind, because it was so unexpected and so strange. In that stopping of the mind is the release. Suddenly the goose is out! Shui Lao became enlightened.

He got up, clapping his hands and laughing loudly, and said, "How extraordinary! How wonderful! Instantly, on the tip of a hair, I have understood the root source of myriad states of concentration, and countless subtle meanings." Then he bowed—in deep respect—and withdrew. Afterward, he would tell the assembly—he became himself a great master—*"From the time I took Ma Tsu's kick, up until now, I have not stopped laughing."*

How can one stop laughing? This great affair is so ridiculous!

It is like a dog who, on a winter morning in the warm sun, sitting silently looking at his tail, becomes interested in catching it. He tries in many ways, and the more he tries, the more he becomes challenged, because the tail jumps immediately. The faster he jumps, the faster the tail jumps—and the difference remains the same. Standing by the side you will laugh: "This stupid dog! That tail belongs to him; there is no need to catch hold of it—and there is no way...."

Your enlightenment belongs to you, there is no need to seek and search. You *are* it. It is not

an achievement, it is only a recognition—hence, the laughter.

Naturally, people who have not been accustomed to the tradition of Zen will be shocked by such behavior. If I suddenly knock somebody over the head here and now, will you understand? You will think, "This man has gone mad." You will think, "We already knew that he was mad; now he has crossed all the boundaries."

But people who are not in a deep resonance with Zen will not be able to understand it—Hindus or Mohammedans or Christians or Jews—because there is nothing like that in their whole history. Their history is more or less intellectual gymnastics.

Zen is absolutely existential. The master is there not only to teach you certain doctrines; he is there to release you from the prison that you yourself have made. Whatever arbitrary, expedient methods are needed, he is not going to be worried about what people will think of them; he will use them.

There have never been more compassionate beings than Zen masters. It is a great compassion of Ma Tsu; otherwise, who cares?—he could have just answered the question and the whole thing would be over. He took so much effort, hit the man, knocked him down....

And it is not only Ma Tsu who is compassionate: Shui Lao also knows tremendous understanding. If it had happened to somebody who was not ready, he would have started fighting or he would have become angry, saying "This is absolutely absurd! I am asking a question and you are hitting me." But he took the hit in the same way as Mahakashyapa had taken the lotus flower from Gautam Buddha—with even more beauty: *"How extraordinary! How wonderful!"*—and with great reverence—... *he bowed down and withdrew.*

No other question... everything is solved. He has been kicked out of the nest; now his wings are open in the sky.

the mystery of
the koan

...the koan of the goose in a bottle. "If a man puts a gosling in a bottle and feeds him until he is full-grown, how can the man get the goose out without killing it or breaking the bottle?"

insoluble puzzles

The very function of the koan is to tire your mind to such a point that it gives up. If there were an answer, the mind would find it. It does not matter whether you are very intelligent, or not very intelligent—no intelligence of any category can find the answer.

ZEN IS NOT a religion, not a dogma, not a creed; Zen is not even a quest, an inquiry; it is non-philosophical. The foundation of the Zen approach is that all is as it should be, nothing is missing. This very moment everything is perfect. The goal is not somewhere else; it is here, it is now. Tomorrows don't exist. This very moment is the only reality. Hence, in Zen there is no distinction between methods and goals, means and ends.

All the philosophies of the world and all the religions of the world create duality; however they may go on talking about non-duality, they create a split personality. That has been the greatest calamity that has befallen humanity: all the do-gooders have created schizophrenia in people. When you divide reality into means and goals, you divide humanity itself, because for humans, the closest reality is themselves.

An individual's consciousness becomes split. He lives here but not really; he is always there, somewhere else. He is always searching, always inquiring; never living, never being. Always doing—getting richer, more powerful, getting spiritual, getting holier, more saintly— always more and more. This constant

hankering for more creates a tense, anguished state; meanwhile he is missing all that is made available by existence. He is interested in the far away, yet God is close by. His eyes are focused on the stars, yet God is within him.

Let me tell you the story of how one of the most famous Zen koans started:

A great and philosophical official, Riko, once asked the strange Zen Master, Nansen, to explain to him the koan of the goose in the bottle.

"If a man puts a gosling into a bottle," said Riko, "and feeds him until he is full-grown, how can the man get the goose out without killing it or breaking the bottle?"

Nansen gave a great clap with his hands and shouted, "Riko!"

"Yes, Master," said the official with a start.

"See," said Nansen, "the goose is out!"

It is only a question of seeing; it is only a question of becoming alert, awake; it is only a question of waking up. The goose is in the bottle if you are in a dream; the goose has never been in the bottle if you are awake. And in the

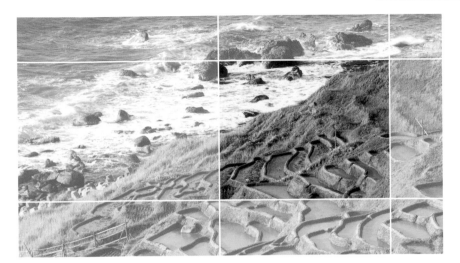

dream there is no way to take the goose out of the bottle. Either the goose will die or the bottle will have to be broken, and neither alternative is allowed. A fully-grown goose in a small bottle.... How can you take it out? This is called a koan.

A koan is not an ordinary puzzle; it is not a puzzle because it cannot be solved. A puzzle is that which has a possibility of being solved; you just have to look for the right answer. You will find it—it only needs intelligence to find the answer to the puzzle; but a puzzle is not insoluble.

A koan is insoluble; you cannot solve it, you can only *dissolve* it. And the way to dissolve it is to change the very plane of your being from dreaming to wakefulness. In the dream the goose is in the bottle and there is no way to bring it out of the bottle without breaking the bottle or killing the goose—in the dream. Hence, as far as the dream is concerned, the

puzzle is impossible; nothing can be done about it. But there is a way out that has nothing to do with the puzzle, remember. You have to wake up. That has nothing to do with the bottle and nothing to do with the goose, either. You have to wake up. It has something to do with *you*. That's why Nansen did not answer the question.

Riko asked, "If a man puts a gosling into a bottle and feeds him until he is full-grown, how can the man get the goose out without killing it or breaking the bottle?"

Nansen didn't answer. On the contrary, he gave a great clap with his hands and shouted, "Riko!"

Now, this is not an answer to the question— this has nothing to do with the question at all— it is irrelevant, inconsistent. But it solves it; in fact, it dissolves it. The moment Nansen shouted, "Riko!" the official, with a start, said,

"Yes, Master." The whole plane of his being was transformed by a simple strategy.

A Zen master is not a teacher; he does not teach you, he simply devises methods to wake you up. That clap is a method; that clap simply brought Riko into the present. And it was so unexpected.... When you are asking such a spiritual koan you don't expect the master to answer you with a loud clap and then to shout your name.

Suddenly Riko was brought out of the past, out of the future. Suddenly for a moment, he forgot the problem. Where is the bottle and where is the goose? There was only the master, in a strange posture, clapping and shouting for Riko. Suddenly the problem was dropped. He had slipped out of the problem without even knowing that he slipped out of it. He had slipped out of the problem as a snake slips out of its old skin. For a moment, time stopped. For a moment, the clock stopped. For a moment, the mind stopped. For a moment, there was nothing. The master, the sound of the clap—and a sudden awakening. In that very moment the master said, "See! See, the goose is out!" it is dissolved.

A koan can only be dissolved but can never be solved. A puzzle can never be dissolved but it can be solved. So remember, a koan is not a puzzle.

When people who are accustomed to continual thinking, to logical reasoning, start studying Zen, they take a false step from the beginning. Zen cannot be studied; it has to be lived; it has to be imbibed—it is a transmission beyond words, a transmission of the lamp. The lamp is invisible.

When you enter into the world of Zen there is no-mind. Zen is equivalent to no-mind. It is not freedom of the mind, it is freedom *from* the mind, and there is a lot of difference, an unbridgeable difference. The mind is not free, you are free of the mind. The mind is no longer there, free or unfree; the mind has simply ceased. You have gone through a new door that was always available to you but you had never knocked on it—the door of being, the door of eternity.

Zen, the very word *zen* comes from the Sanskrit word *dhyana*. *Dhyana* means "meditation," but the word *meditation* does not carry its total significance. *Meditation* gives the impression that mind is doing something: mind meditating, concentrating, contemplating, but mind is there. *Dhyana* means a state of no-mind—no concentration, no contemplation, no meditation, in fact—just silence, a deep, profound silence where all thoughts have disappeared. When there is no ripple in the lake of consciousness; the consciousness is functioning just like a mirror reflecting all that is—the stars, the trees, the birds, the people, all that is—simply reflecting it without any distortion, without any interpretation, without bringing in any prejudices.

That's what your mind is: your prejudices, your ideologies, your dogmas, your habits. Mind can never be free. Freedom and mind never meet. Mind means bondage; mind is a prison. In the mind you live an encapsulated life, surrounded by all kinds of thoughts, theories, systems, philosophies, the history of humanity, all kinds of superstitions—Hindu,

Mohammedan, Christian, Buddhist, Jaina, political, social, economic, religious. Either your mind is made up of the bricks of the Bible, the Koran, the Gita...or maybe *Das Kapital* or the *Communist Manifesto*. You may have made your prison differently from others, you may have chosen a different architect, but the prison is the same.

The architect can be Sigmund Freud, Karl Marx, Albert Einstein—you can choose: prisons come in all shapes and all sizes and the interior decoration is up to you. You can put beautiful paintings inside, you can carpet it wall to wall, you can paint it according to your likes and dislikes. You can make a few changes here and there, a window on the left or on the right,

a curtain of this material or that. But a prison is a prison. Mind *as such* is a prison, and everybody is living in a prison. Unless you get out of the prison you will never know what freedom is. Your prison can be cozy, comfortable, convenient; it can be well decorated, golden, studded with diamonds, and it will be difficult to leave it. You have worked so hard to create it, it is not going to be easy. But a prison is a prison; made of gold or made of mud, it makes no difference. You will never know the infinity of freedom; you will never know the beauty and the splendor of freedom; your splendor will die in the bottle. You will never know that the goose is always out.

zen in
the west

People in the West who have written about Zen don't know

what effort Zen people have been making before they relax.

Much has to be done before you can come to a point where

relaxation is possible. And that relaxation is not from you—

it happens: because the whole energy has moved, nothing

remains behind to be restless; a rest comes.

a new approach to existence

People are translating Zen books, people are commenting on Zen books, but all their commentaries and all their talks about Zen are intellectual. They are fed up with Christianity and they are in search of something fresh and new, but although they have found in Zen fresh insights, their approach remains Western, the approach of intellect. Their approach remains Socratic, Aristotelian. They are beautiful people, but their Zen is only a mind phenomenon; they have not experienced it. It is not their own truth; they have borrowed it from different sources.

THE WESTERN intelligentsia have become acquainted with Zen, have even fallen in love with Zen, but they are still trying to approach Zen from the mind. They have not yet come to the understanding that Zen has nothing to do with mind. Its tremendous job is to get you out of the prison of the mind. It is not an intellectual philosophy. It is not a philosophy at all. Nor is it a religion, because it has no fictions, no lies, no consolations. It is a lion's roar. The greatest thing that Zen has brought into the world is freedom from oneself.

All the religions have been talking about dropping your ego. But it is a weird phenomenon: they want you to drop your ego, and the ego is just a shadow of God. God is the ego of the universe, and the ego is your personality. Just as God is the center of existence according to religions, your ego is the center of your mind, of your personality. They have all been talking about dropping the ego, but it cannot be dropped unless God is dropped. You cannot drop a shadow or a reflection unless the source of its manifestation is destroyed.

So religions have been saying continuously, for centuries, that you should get rid of the ego—but for wrong reasons. They have been asking you to drop your ego so you can surrender to God, so you can surrender to the priests, so you can surrender to any kind of nonsense, any kind of theology, superstition, belief system.

Zen goes beyond the ego and beyond the self. Except Zen, no religion has come to the point of going beyond the self, beyond your spirit, beyond your individuality. Zen is essentially freedom from oneself. You have heard about other freedoms, but freedom from oneself is the ultimate freedom—not to be, and

to allow existence to express itself in all its spontaneity and grandeur. But it is existence— not you, not me. It is life itself dancing—not you, not me.

Only Zen has refined, in these twenty-five centuries, methods and devices to make you aware that you are not, that you are only arbitrary, just an idea.

As you go beyond the mind, even the idea of "I am" disappears. When the "I" also disappears and you start feeling a deep involvement in existence, with no boundaries, only then has Zen blossomed in you.

In fact, that is the state, the space of the awakened consciousness. But it has no "I" at the center.

To make it clear to you, Socrates says, "Know thyself." Gautam Buddha says, "Know—just know, and you will not find thyself." Enter deeper into your awareness, and the deeper you go, your self starts melting. Perhaps that is the reason why none of the religions except Zen have tried meditation— because meditation will destroy God, will

destroy the ego, will destroy the self. It will leave you in absolute nothingness. It is only the mind that makes you afraid of nothingness. I receive this question almost every day: "Why are we afraid of nothingness?" You are afraid because you don't know nothingness. You are afraid only because you figure out intellectually,

"What is the point? If in meditation you have to disappear, then it is better to remain in the mind." At least you *are*—maybe illusory, maybe just an idea, but at least you are. What is the point of making all this effortless effort just to disappear into nothingness?

The mind makes you reluctant to go beyond the boundaries of the mind, because beyond the boundaries of the mind you will exist no more. That will be the ultimate death.

A Gautam Buddha dies ultimately, you die only temporarily. Maybe a few minutes, a few seconds, and you enter into another womb. Some idiots are always making love around the world, twenty-four hours, and you don't have to travel far away, just in the neighborhood.

Around the clock millions of couples are making love, so whichever is the closest couple, here you die and there you are born. The gap is very small.

Mind is afraid, and it seems logical, obvious: What is the point? Why should one do such a thing in which he disappears?

Gautam Buddha was told again and again, "You are a strange fellow. We came here to realize our self, and your meditation is to *un*realize our self."

Socrates was a great genius, but confined to the mind: "Know thyself." There is no self to be known. That is the Zen message to the world. There is nothing to know. You have only to be one with the whole. There is no need to be afraid....

Think for a moment: When you were not born, was there any anxiety, any worry, any angst? You were not there, there was no problem. You are the problem, the beginning of the problem, and as you grow, more and more problems.... But before your birth, was there any problem?

Zen masters continuously ask the newcomers, "Where were you before your father was born?" An absurd question, but of immense significance. They are asking you, "If you were not, there was no problem. So what is the worry?" If your death becomes the ultimate death and all boundaries disappear, you will not be there, but the existence will be there. The dance will be there, but the dancer will not be there. The song will be there, but the singer will not be there.

This is only possible to experience by falling deeper, beyond the mind, to the very depth of your being, to the very source of life from where your life is flowing. Suddenly you realize the image of yourself was arbitrary. You are imageless; you are infinite. You were living in a cage. The moment you realize your sources are infinite, the cage disappears and you can open your wings into the blue sky and disappear. This disappearance is freedom from oneself. But this is possible not through intellect, it is possible only through meditation. Zen is another name for meditation.

Hundreds of beautiful books have appeared in the West since a strange man, D.T. Suzuki, introduced Zen to the West. He did a pioneer job, but he was not a Zen master, or even a man of Zen. He was a great scholar, and his impact spread through all the countries to the intelligentsia. He immediately had great appeal.

The old religions are crumbling, particularly in the West. Christianity is just a name; the empire is crumbling. They are trying to hold onto it, but it is not possible. This creates a great anxiety: "We are worthless...nobody needs us...existence doesn't care." At that moment D.T. Suzuki appeared on the horizon in the West. He was the first man to talk about Zen in the Western universities and colleges, and his work was immensely attractive to intelligent people, because they had lost faith in organized religions.

D.T. Suzuki appeared in the West with a new approach to existence. He appealed to people because he was a man of great scholarship, profound scholarship, and he brought to the Western mind a new concept of religion. But it

remained a concept; it remained an argument in the mind; it never went deeper than that.

A parallel exists in China. Before Bodhidharma appeared in China, China was already converted to Buddhism. Bodhidharma went there fourteen hundred years ago, but Gautam Buddha's philosophy and religion had reached China two thousand years ago, six hundred years before Bodhidharma went there. In those six hundred years scholars had converted the whole of China to Buddhism.

In those days it was easy to convert the whole country. You simply converted the emperor, and then his whole court was converted, then his whole army was converted, then his whole bureaucracy was converted. And when the emperor and the whole bureaucracy and the army and all the so-called wise people of the emperor's court were converted, the masses simply followed.

The masses have never decided anything for themselves. They simply follow the people who proclaim themselves great, in power, in intelligence, in riches. If these people are converted, the masses simply follow.

So in those six hundred years, thousands of Buddhist scholars reached China and converted China—the emperors, the governors. But it was not the true message of Gautam Buddha yet. Although China had become Buddhist, Buddha had not yet appeared. Bodhidharma was sent by his master, who was a woman. She said, "Scholars have prepared the way, now you go. You are immensely needed there." Bodhidharma was the first buddha to enter China, and he brought a totally different vision, not of the mind but of no-mind. For six hundred years in China, Buddhism had been only an intellectual exercise, good gymnastics. But as Bodhidharma entered China, he changed the whole idea about Zen.

❝ Zen means to be so alone that there is nothing to meditate upon. No object, just simple subjectivity exists— consciousness without clouds, a pure sky ❞

People were talking about Zen as if it were another philosophy, which it is not; as if it were another religion, which it is not. It is a rebellion against mind, and all your religions and philosophies are part of the mind.

This is the only rebellion against mind, against self, the only rebellion of withdrawing all the limits that imprison you and taking a quantum leap into nothingness. But this nothingness is very alive. It is life; it is existence. It is not a hypothesis. And when you take the jump, the first experience is that you are disappearing. The last experience is that you have become the whole.

Why have so many Western intellectuals been drawn to an examination of Zen? They are feeling a great vacuum, and they want to fill it. You cannot live with a vacuum. The vacuum is empty, and out of that emptiness, life becomes sad, serious.

All the religions have been filling your vacuum with lies. Now those lies are exposed. Science has done much in exposing those lies, and great meditators and mystics, have done tremendous work around the world in exposing the lies of religions.

The contemporary person stands in a strange position: the old has fallen, it was a deception, and the new has not yet arrived. So there is a gap, an interval, and the Western intelligentsia is trying to find something which will not be a lie, which will not just give you consolation, but which will transform you, which will be a deep revolution in your being.

Zen certainly is the right approach toward existence, the ultimate truth. Without believing in anything, without being a follower or a believer, you enter into your own interiority and into the immense nothingness of the whole. It is the same nothingness from where you have come and to where you are going again.

When the source and the goal become one, you will have a great celebration. In that celebration you will not be, but all of existence will be participating. The trees will be showering flowers, the birds will be singing songs, and the oceans and the rivers will all be rejoicing.

The whole existence becomes your home the moment your heart melts into the universal heart. That is where Zen is happening. In that melting into the universe, you are back to the

as sweet, but if you have not tasted sugar, you hear the word *sweet* but don't understand what it is. The only way is for somebody to put some sweetness into your mouth.

The master's function in Zen is to force nothingness into your experience or, in other words, to bring you to your own nothingness. The master devises methods and when they become old and routine he drops them, finds new methods, new ways.

It has been twenty-five centuries since Gautam Buddha gave a lotus flower to Mahakashyapa, without a single word, and told his congregation, "What I could say I have told you. What I cannot say—although I want to, but it is simply not possible—I am transferring to Mahakashyapa." That lotus flower was a symbol: unless you open up like a lotus flower in the early morning sun when the dewdrops are shining like pearls on the lotus leaves.... It is a silent transmission of the lamp. Nothing is said.

Mahakashyapa came for the first time close to Buddha, took the lotus flower, touched his feet, went back and sat silently under his tree. Mahakashyapa is the first patriarch of Zen. So the lineage of Zen, the family of Zen, is a branch, a silent branch of Buddhism. They love Gautam Buddha, because Zen really originated in his disappearance. He transferred it to Mahakashyapa, and then it was the responsibility of Mahakashyapa to go on finding people to whom he could transfer it.

So since that moment, twenty-five centuries ago, it has been transferred without any

original source, fresh, eternal, timeless, spacious. The only thing needed is freedom from the self. That is the essence of Zen. You have heard about many freedoms: political freedom, psychological freedom, economic freedom—there are many kinds of freedom. The ultimate freedom is Zen, freedom from yourself. That is not to be accepted as a belief, it has to be experienced. Only then will you know. It is a taste. Anybody can describe sugar

arbitrary means, without any language, from master to disciple; from one who has come home to one who is just wandering around and cannot find the way.

The master functions as a friend. He holds your hand and takes you on the right path, helps you to open your eyes, helps you become capable of transcending the mind. That's when your third eye opens, when you start looking inward. Once you are looking inward, the master's work is finished. Now it is up to you.

You can travel that small gap between your mind and no-mind in a single moment of tremendous intensity and urgency. Or you can travel slowly, hesitantly, stopping, being afraid that you are losing grip of your mind, you are losing grip of your individuality, that all boundaries are disappearing. What are you doing? You may think for a moment, "This may bring a breakdown, I may not be able to come back to my mind again. And who knows what is going to happen ahead? Things are disappearing...."

If you pay too much attention to the things that are disappearing, you may stop out of fear. The master helps you focus your mind on things that are happening, not on things that are disappearing. He forces you to look at the blissfulness, at the silence that is descending on you. Look at the peace, look at the joy, look at the ecstasy. He continuously emphasizes that which is happening, not that which is going away—the anxiety, the despair, the angst, the anguish; he does not allow you even to take note of them. What is disappearing is not worth keeping. Keep looking at what is appearing out of nothingness.

So you gather courage, you become more daring. You know that nothing is going to be wrong. With every single inch of movement, something greater is happening. Finally, as you enter the source of your being, the center of your being, the universe falls upon you, as if the whole ocean has fallen into a dewdrop.

Once you have experienced this beatitude, this ecstasy, this divine drunkenness, who cares about individuality? Who cares about the self? What has the self given to you except anxiety, except hell? And this nothingness is so pure, without boundaries. For the first time you find the infinity, the eternity, and all the mysteries of existence are suddenly opening their doors to you. And they go on opening... door after door....

There is no end to this journey; it is an endless pilgrimage. You are always arriving and arriving and arriving, but you never arrive. Each moment you are going deeper into bliss, deeper into ecstasy, deeper into truth, and there is no full stop.

> *There is no end to this journey; it is an endless pilgrimage. You are always arriving and arriving and arriving, but you never arrive*

A Zen Manifesto is absolutely needed, because old religions are falling apart, and before they fall apart and humanity goes completely bananas, Zen has to be spread wide around the earth. Before the old house falls down, you have to create a new house.

And this time don't commit the same mistake. You have been living in a house which was not there; hence, you were suffering rain, winter, sun, because the house was imaginary. This time enter into your original home, not into any man-made temple, any man-made religion. Enter into your own existence. Why be continuously a carbon copy?

This time is valuable. You are born in a fortunate moment, when the old has lost its validity, its proof, when the old is simply hanging around you because you are not courageous enough to get out of the prison. Otherwise, the doors are open—in fact, there have never been any doors, because the house you are living in is completely imaginary. Your gods are imaginary, your priests are imaginary, your holy scriptures are imaginary. This time don't commit the same mistake. This time humanity has to take a quantum leap from the old rotten lies to the fresh, eternally fresh truth.

This is the Manifesto of Zen. D.T. Suzuki said, "Zen must be seized with bare hands, with no gloves on." His statement is rationally beautiful. You should seize Zen with your bare, naked hands, with no gloves on. He means that you should enter into the world of

Zen without any beliefs, without any security, without any safety, without any gloves. You should enter into Zen with naked hands, with nudity.

But his statement is still intellectual. He was neither a master of Zen nor even a man of Zen. If he had been a master of Zen, he could not have said it. A master of Zen cannot say that Zen must be seized. It is not a question of seizing Zen. This is the old language of the mind, of "conquering nature." Now it becomes conquering Zen.

Zen is your reality. Whom are you going to seize? Whom are you going to conquer? You *are* Zen.

And what does he mean by "with bare hands"? Hands will not reach there, bare or with gloves on. Hands symbolize movement outward; they always point toward the outside. All your senses open to the outside; they are all extrovert. Your ears hear the sound that is coming from the outside, your eyes see colors, light that is coming from the outside, your hand goes on grabbing—that is outside you. None of your senses can reach to the inside. For the inside there is a different sensitivity, the third eye. There are no hands.

Just between your two eyebrows, exactly in the middle, is the place which can look inward. When you are with closed eyes, trying to look inward, rushing toward your center, you are hitting on the third eye continuously. Because it has not been opened for centuries, it has forgotten how to open.

There are no hands, and there is no question of conquering. It is your nature. The very idea

that Zen must be seized creates a duality: you are the person who is going to seize Zen, and Zen is something other than you. It creates a duality. That's what gives me a clear-cut idea whether the person is intellectualizing or has had the experience.

Mind is dual; it always divides things into polar opposites: the conqueror and the conquered, the observer and the observed, the object and the subject, the day and the night. It divides things that are not divided. Neither is the day divided from the night, nor is birth divided from death. They are one energy. But mind goes on dividing everything into polarities, opposites. Nothing is opposite in existence; every contradiction is only apparent. Deep down all contradictions are meeting together.

So when somebody says, "Seize, conquer," he is still talking in the language of the mind and is still being violent. The words show it.

Zen has to be neither the object nor the subject. It is a transcendental experience. Duality of all kinds is transcended: the observer and the observed become one, the knower and the known become one. So it is not a question of conquering or seizing, it is a question of relaxing into yourself.

It is not a fight or a war, it is pure resting, sinking into your rest deeply. And as you sink deeper and deeper you find you are melting. The moment you come to oneness with existence, you have arrived at your nature. It can be possible only through relaxation, through rest.

Zen is the only existential approach in the world.

afterword

ZEN IS LIKE a telegram. Have you noticed that when you write a letter, it becomes longer and longer? It is easy to start the letter but difficult to end it. When you send a telegram, just ten words, it is a condensed message. Your ten-page-long letter will not have the same effect as the ten words of a telegram. The more condensed the meaning, the more striking. The more spread the meaning, the less impressive.

Zen believes in the essentials. It has no nonsense around it; no rituals, in which all other religions have got lost; no chanting, no mantras, no scriptures—just small anecdotes. If you have the right awareness, they will hit you directly in the heart. It is a condensed and crystallized teaching, but a person must be prepared for it. The only preparation is meditative awareness.

You cannot teach Zen in universities for the simple reason that the students don't have meditative awareness, and there are no books on Zen that can make meaningful that which looks absurd.

You will be surprised that in many Zen universities they are teaching Zen through my books, because my books at least make an effort to make the absurd appear sensible.

I try to provide a context and the right background for those who are not born in the Zen tradition. Zen books themselves are fragmentary. They are telegrams—urgent, immediate, not giving any explanation, but simply giving the essence, the perfume of thousands of flowers. You have to be alert and meditative to absorb them.

If you can absorb them, in the world's literature there is nothing more important than Zen anecdotes. In everything they are unique. They are small paintings, and just watching them, you will fall into such peace.

There are great poetries, but not of the same significance as the small haikus from Zen. I have always loved Basho, one of the haiku masters. His haikus say so much that even a thousand-page holy scripture does not say—it is all so much prose. A haiku of Basho is:

The ancient pond...

When you hear the haiku, you have to visualize it. It is so small that it is not a question of understanding, it is a question of entering into it. *The ancient pond...* Experience the feel of an ancient pond, visualize it.

The ancient pond
A frog jumps in
Plop

And the haiku is complete.

But Basho has said so much: the ancient pond, the ancient trees, the ancient rocks around it.... and there must be silence.... and a frog jumps in. For a moment the silence is disturbed, *plop*. And again the silence is restored.... perhaps deeper than it was before. What does he want to say in this haiku? He is saying, This ancient world...and your existence is just a *plop*, a little sound in the silence. And then you are gone, and the silence deepens. In this way he makes the whole world ephemeral, dreamlike—nothing solid in it, only great silence.

That great silence is your very being. It is also the very being of the whole universe.

about Osho

Osho is a contemporary mystic whose teachings have inspired millions of people from all walks of life. His works, which are published in more than 40 languages, are transcribed from extemporaneous talks given over a period of 35 years. They cover everything from the individual search for happiness to the most pressing social, political, and spiritual concerns of our time. *The Sunday Times* of London has named Osho as one of the "1000 Makers of the 20th Century." His books are bestsellers in many languages and many countries. There are more than thirty original books by Osho on Zen and Zen masters. Many of them are available in different languages:

Osho Zen Tarot—The Transcendental Game of Zen (card deck plus book)

The Search (On the Ten Bulls of Zen)

For the availability of editions in different languages, check the Osho website.

More about OSHO

For more information about Osho, see www.osho.com—a comprehensive website in several languages with information about the author, his work, and the Osho Meditation Resort.

Located 100 miles southeast of Mumbai in the thriving modern city of Pune, India, the OSHO International Meditation Resort is a holiday destination with a difference. The Meditation Resort is spread over 28 acres of spectacular gardens in a beautiful tree-lined residential area.

www.osho.com/meditationresort

www.osho.com/guesthouse

www.osho.com/livingin